Housekeeping Management

HOUSEKEEPING MANAGEMENT

DR. D.K. Aggarwal

PRINCIPAL
INSTITUTE OF HOTEL MANAGEMENT &
CATERING TECHNOLOGY
BHOPAL (M.P.)

AMAN PUBLICATIONS
NEW DELHI (INDIA)

Published by
Rajiv Jain for Aman Publications
LG-4A, Ganpati Bhawan,
4675-B/21, Ansari Road,
Darya Ganj, Delhi - 110002
PH: 23255012, 23282127
E-mail: sshjbs@yahoo.com

Reprinted 2022

ISBN-81-8204-023-X (HB)

SOLE DISTRIBUTOR
JINDAL BOOK SERVICES
LG-4A, Ganpati Bhawan,
4675-B/21, Ansari Road,
Darya Ganj, Delhi - 110002

Laser Typesetting by:
S.M. Graphics, Delhi,

Printed by:
NCT Printers & Publishers , Delhi, India

Preface

Housekeeping is the maintenance of a clean environment, usually in a house, but it also applies to industrial, commercial, and institutional settings. A well-run housekeeping department is integral to the success of any lodging operation. Good housekeeping provides a clean and pleasant lodging environment. It can usually be achieved by routine cleaning of the premises, proper storage of materials, periodic disposal of rubbish, regular maintenance of facilities and full staff co-operation.

Management of a housekeeping operation entails scheduling staff, deliveries, services and maintenance, budget analysis, cost-controls and compliance with regulations. Today, the ideal executive housekeeper must be prepared to be a first-line manager—capable of running a housekeeping department with little or no intervention from upper management.

This book offers future industry professionals the tools they need to be competitive in this new era—the skills to manage resources, administer assets, and manage all of the technical operations of a busy housekeeping department. It will be an invaluable resource for all who need to succeed in the hospitality industry.

CONTENTS

1

Philosophy of Housekeeping

Every household arrangement must differ in detail—in way and modes of living as well as in numbers. No amount of love, of beauty, or of intelligence will make home happy without a "right judgement" on the part of the housewife. A woman must rule her household, or be ruled by it; she must either hold the reins with a tight, firm hand, never parting with, but seldom using, the whip; or the reins fall from the idle, careless hand, and are seized by subordinates, and the hard-working husband is placed, by his wife's indolence, under the control of his domestics, and has to depend upon their honesty and zeal alone.

Early rising on the part of the mistress is even more essential than for the servants to the early risers; for if the maids see that the mistress does not stir at an early hour, they think that they may indulge a little too: but if their mistress be regular in making her appearance, the maids do not like a good, kind lady to have cheerless, undusted rooms to go into, and take care to be in good time.

If a mother, with a young infant, if she should don a dressing-gown in place of a dress, and wash her baby before coming down; indeed, if children of any age take morning baths, we advocate that no one but *mamma* should dry them. As soon as these duties are over, the mistress should proceed to the breakfast-room and make the tea, coffee, or chocolate, and ring be bell for the breakfast, as above stated. When it is possible to get the master to enjoy an eight o'clock breakfast, household matters go on charmingly. He is usually out of the house by nine, and by that hour the windows are wide open, every door set open (weather permitting), and a thorough draught of "delicious air" is passed through the whole dwelling.

The work of the household will proceed with a far greater regularity and despatch when the mistress is able and willing to assist in the lighter duties. The first duty of the mistress after breakfast is to give her orders for the day, and she naturally begins with the cook. If a servant find that her mistress is determined to see for herself that her orders involve no extravagance and no waste, she will do one of two things—either enter fully into her mistresse's views, or leave her place. Both courses are good for the mistress, but naturally the first is the pleasanter to all parties.

Young wives are often lonely and talk to their maids for a change; it is a bad plan, depend upon it, and often causes disagreeable liberties to be taken. The mistress should carefully inspect every portion of the room, as it is her careful and observant eye alone that will detect careless or unhealthy habits in her maids.

Windows should look bright and clean; no dust should deface the furniture, or thread or speck the carpet; all water-vessels should be clean, and filled with pure water: a small quantity of hot water should be placed in the chamber utensils. The towels should be taken out to air in the garden, weather permitting, or dried in the kitchen.

The bed should look neat, the counterpane being smoothly drawn over it, and curtains arranged in seemly folds. The blinds should hang evenly, and the window curtains be neatly looped back.

The closest inspection should be made of every room in the house, not excepting the very smallest; and nothing should be omitted to be placed where required. Bedroom, clothes, and other closets should be kept scrupulously clean, and everything wanted should be put ready to hand. Water supplies and drains should be carefully and regularly supervised, and newspaper, it should be remembered, is apt to stop up the drain and cause much expense, which curling-paper does not. The mistress should ascertain that the water supply is plentiful, for it is on these apparent trifles that the health of households depends.

The garden should now be inspected, and orders given to the gardener, and the plants in the house attended to by the lady. As it is good for the maids to have a settled plan of their work, so it is good for the mistress to arrange her day, by rule, as far as possible. Interruptions will occur from time to time, but a resolute woman will generally carry out her plans for the week satisfactorily.

Minor details of housework should be attended to by the mistress, who should see that her servants attend to the little things that give a neat and cared-for appearance to the house. For example, the doorsteps must be cleaned and whitened daily; the blinds drawn down and shutters closed regularly as soon as it is dark; all windows closed at sunset, and opened as soon as possible in the morning.

The mistress must look at the outside of her house as well as see that the inside is all right. She should survey her house on all sides from a little distance, and note if it is as nice as she could wish in respect to repairs, arrangement of curtains, blinds etc. The forecourt and garden also must the trim and neat, if not gay with flowers. Periodically the roof and gutters should be examined, and all refuse matter removed, and free passage given for the rain-water.

Keeping Linen Press

Good linen, though expensive, is far more economical than is cheap linen. Sheets should be wider and longer than their bed they are used on, and should be marked in pairs. The hems should be sewn, not hemmed, with linen thread.

Pillow-cases should be of fine linen, the cases to fit easily the pillows, and made with a double hem, in which button-holes are placed. Finely-frilled pillow-cases look very nice, but unless expense is of little object, should be kept for the use of the spare room. Pillow-cases should be arranged in half-dozens, and an elastic band and card placed round each parcel, with the mark, number, and room to which they belong clearly written on the card.

Table cloths should be folded carefully, and each table-cloth should have the band and card, with the mark, date, etc.., and, in addition, the size of the table-cloth. For by this plan the size is known at a glance, and so trouble and loss of time in unfolding and refolding avoided.

Table napkins should not be marked in ink, but the monogram worked in raised embroidery. These are usually kept in a silk case, but may be tied by tapes, on which a card describing them is sewn; as, for instance, "Dinner" or "Breakfast," "Dinner, best," "Dinner, daily."

Towels should be arranged in the same way as the other parcels of linen; the elastic band and card are convenient for these; they should be arranged in half-dozens, whether rough, bath, fine, or of medium quality.

Bathe sheets are far pleasanter to use than ordinary towels. They should be of fine huckabuck, and measure three yards each way; better still if the length is allowed another half-yard. They should be dried daily, and brought in hot at the hour for rising. On leaving the bath, one is entirely enveloped in the warm sheet, and the process of drying is conducted with rapidity and comfort.

Servants' sheets, pillow-cases, towels etc., should all be arranged in the same manner, and attended to with equal care; they should be given out when required by the mistress, who should have all changes of bed-linen made with exact regularity. The old-fashioned plan was to change the upper-sheet every fortnight, giving a clean upper-sheet, and taking the upper-sheet in place of the lower. This plan insures regularity of wear in the sheets.

Glass cloths should be of good linen; that sold for white roller blinds answers admirably, as it is soft, without fluff, and is not expensive.

Tea cloths are of coarser linen, but very coarse cloths are not economical, as they are clumsy, and often cause breakages.

Kitchen cloths— Round towels are made of coarse linen, and what is called "Crash," respectively. A good supply of these is required in every house.

Dusters are sold at prices varying from sixpence to a shilling each, but are far more effective when made of old chintz, old linings, etc., being softer, and taking up the dust far better than the dressed stiff linen. Ugly, old-fashioned chintz is often sold at threepence and fourpence a yard, and when washed, makes admirable dusters at this low price.

Every mistress who wishes to preserve her kitchen cloths from holes and burns will provide a kettle-holder for the kitchen, and a pot and saucepan-holder; these may be bought at the door for threepence, or, made out of old pieces, will save many a good cloth and duster from being burned, made dirty, or destroyed.

Housekeeping Accounts

One of the greatest trials of the young wife is the account-book. This book becomes a perfect bugbear to some ladies, who are yet perfectly capable of keeping a neat and regular debtor and creditor account if they could be once started with a regular system of account-keeping.

Girls, whose monetary responsibilities have begun and ended with their quarterly allowance, find housekeeping accounts very difficult to manage properly; and although experienced matrons may smile that these words, a lesson in easy account-keeping is not without value.

A neatly-bound account book of oblong shape, an ivory slate and pencil, and a card and pencil in the purse is the whole stock-in-trade as account-keeper. The account-book is kept in the mistress's Davenport, the slate hangs up in the kitchen, and the card and purse are naturally in the pocket.

Every time any money is spent enter the item at once on the card, which is kept in place in the purse by an elastic passed offer it. Every Saturday remove the card and insert a fresh one, copying the list on the card into the account-book.

Every Saturday morning receive the household books from the cook, who hands the slate, on which she has marked the sums paid at the kitchen door for parcels and sundries not put down in the weekly books; this statement includes all extras. Then copy the sums written on the sheet into the weekly account-book, of which we subjoin a specimen page. It will be observed that we "enter," or write down the sums paid out on the right-hand page only, reserving the left-hand page for sums received.

Each double page is complete in itself. And the end of every quarter or thirteen weeks enter the total of sums received and paid, giving the dates of each week, as above shown. It will be seen that the balance of each week is shown on the week's account, and the quarterly balance is struck on the page which shows the quarter's total expenses.

Every week you put down extra expenses, as taxes, or wages (for which a cheque or money order is received), on the right hand page, entering in the same line on the *left* -hand page the check for taxes, wages, etc., or whatever the item is; thus the actual expense is shown each week, independently of all sums given and paid for extras other than housekeeping.

But account-keeping does not begin and end with the account-book. Every tradesman's book should be compared with the cook's slate or tally, or tickets brought with the meat, as in the butcher's case, for instance; then the books must be added up, or the statements verified by the ready-reckoner, as few ladies are clever enough to keep reckoning tables in their heads as one does the multiplication tables.

The meat tickets should be kept on a hook in the kitchen, and verified by the mistress when comparing the weight charged with that sent in. The cook most of course weigh the meat before allowing the butcher to leave the door; she will then be able to see if the weight is correct, and make the butcher alter the ticket or take back the joint if the weight is not correct. Groceries must also be weighed, as well as bread, and, indeed, all goods sold by weight. Washing should be counted over by the housemaid on Monday morning in presence of the mistress, who should enter the items in the washing-book, and, on the return of the linen, the housemaid should compare the quantities returned with the book before airing and putting the linen away.

Daily Duties of Servants

The beds are stripped, and slops emptied in all the rooms. Then bed-making follows; then the sitting-room not used for breakfast must be swept, dusted, and arranged; and then the routine cleaning of the day must follow. Every household has good reasons for each day's work.

The nurse cleans her own nursery, night nursery, and her own bedroom. The COOK undertakes steps and hall, passages, kitchen, larder, scullery, and washhouse, and downstairs closets, and, by arrangement with the mistress at time of hiring, cleans the dining-room and helps to make the beds.

Window-cleaning is also a matter of special arrangement. The cook "answers the door" until 12 o'clock, after which hour the housemaid is supposed to be dressed, and should be, if she is quick and clever at her work. The cook should clean her own bedroom, even if shared by the housemaid; and the housemaid is bound, by kitchen etiquette, the unspoken tradition of the spit, to make the tea at breakfast, to arrange and make tea at the afternoon meal, and to lay the cloth for the kitchen supper. This rule has originated, no doubt, in the kindly feeling which prompts those who have no cooking to do to prepare the meals for those whose work is almost entirely cooking, and who are, therefore, little disposed to do so for themselves.

It is well, when engaging servants, to mention all the rules that a mistress considers best for the happiness of her household, and these details cannot be too much studied by those who hold the reins. A holiday every six weeks should be given to each servant, and by turns they should be allowed to go out on Sunday evenings. Some families can manage to allow one maid the Sunday morning, the other the Sunday evening, but this cannot always be done.

If servants work hard they require some ale, and by providing a cask of good ale, and putting it in the cook's charge, they have sufficient, and there is no objectionable calling of public-house boys for orders or beer-cans. The ale should be computed to last a certain time, and the brewer be ordered to call at regular intervals. Women servants are allowed a pint and men servants a quart per diem, and a gallon over should be allowed in small households for waste in constant drawing. The family, if ale-drinkers, should have a separate cask, as it is impossible to ascertain the right quantity to be used when friends drop in.

Servants should never be reproved before each other or before anyone. If there is occasion for more than a word of direction, a lady should ring for her servant and speak kindly and seriously to her, showing a willingness to help her, though by no means slighting over the subject in question, or allowing any timidity of demeanour to appear.

Domestic quarrels often embitter the peace of households and cause dismissals; these can be quelled by a gentle firmness and the following rules:— never listen to what one servant says of another; never ask a question about a new comer of the old trusted servant; if angry voices and loud talk reach your ear, ring for the delinquents, and before *both* say, "I have no wish to interfere with your quarrels; say and do what you please; but *I* must never hear a sound of dispute or anger in this house." The utter absurdity of being *allowed* to quarrel will, in most cases, prevent a repetition of the offence; and as this is a tried recipe for domestic *broils*, we give it verbatim.

If a lady will reflect upon the importance of engaging a good servant, she will hesitate before taking a written character, unless under very exceptional circumstances. There are four ways of obtaining servants : inquiring of trades-persons; advertising for servants; answering advertisements; and applying at servants' offices.

When servants are obtained through tradesmen, which is one of the easiest modes, there are some disadvantages. The servant is placed under favour to her patron, and in case of a dishonest butcher, for example, would be expected to shut her eyes to short weights, inferior meat, etc. Then she frequently has acquaintances in the neighbourhood, or has been servant to some of one's friends: two objections to begin with, and many others will suggest themselves. Advertising for servants costs from three to five shillings, according to the length of advertisement, and entails remaining at home during the hours stated.

This, where practicable, is an excellent plan, for when the lady sees a servant whose appearance pleases her, whose recommendations are apparently good, and whose "character" is not "short," she can enter into details of the work, show the servant the house, the rooms, and ascertain whether the arrangements, if carried out, are likely to be permanent. The servant, on her side, can judge of the kind of place and mistress, and decide for or against it at once, instead of in a "month's time."

Applying at servants' offices and homes is one of the best plans; and at some of these, ladies can comfortably see and engage servants. The characters are all inspected by the managers; but as, with so large a number, the minute points which so particularly affect the comfort of a household cannot be determined, a mistress should never think any trouble too great which allows a personal interview with the late mistress of the proposed maid.

Gentleness, kindness, and firmness are the qualities required in a mistress, with a thorough practical knowledge of what are her servants' duties. We may here remark that those households are best conducted where the mistress never converses with her servants; never speaks but to gently give an order, ask a question, or say good morning and evening to her maids. Of course, this does not apply in times of sorrow for the servants, or with a general servant, who is depending on her mistress for all occasions of speaking, or to old, well-tried servants, but it is a safe rule for the mistress.

When two servants are kept, the mistress has more time at her disposal, but should nevertheless take a close and watchful interest in the work of the house, inspecting the work when finished, and remarking on badly-cleaned rooms, neglected corners, and seeing that the fault is repaired at the moment. By never passing over a fault during the first twelve months, but kindly and gently pointing it out, there will be no need for a word of correction afterwards.

When servants first enter a service they naturally try their best to please, and require only teaching the "ways" of the family. They soon see if the "missus" is "particular" or no, and whether they are ruled by a careful, clever hand, or by a careless, idle, anyhow mistress, and will act accordingly.

If waste is allowed to run riot in a household,— if articles of daily food are wasted, badly *bought*, badly cooked, badly carved, and made the *least* of,-- there will be no funds left in the mistress's hands with which to pay for the doctor her kindness would call in to her sick servant. Care and thrift mean *power to help others;* economy in daily life permits good actions in life's trials. Good housewifery comprises the duty of woman. Pages might be written upon this subject, but a few hints will suffice to prove this to a thoughtful woman.

The washing of a family should be put out where one servant alone is kept, as we have stated; but many clever managers find time to do all the family washing at home, and yet are not "in a muddle," as it is expressively termed, upon washing-day; the damping, folding, and ironing being done by the mistress, the hard labour by the maid. With the help of one of Bradford's washing-machines this labour is much reduced, and the wringer and mangle are equally handy.

In the evening the mistress should only make the tea and attend to her husband; the last thing at night she should inspect the doors and the whole of the basement, noting every want of cleanliness in the scullery or wash-house, and ascertaining that all be secure, and the plate in her room before she retires to rest, which should be not later than eleven o'clock; for unless she is allowed a certain season of rest, it is impossible for a woman, however willing, to rise at seven, and fill the innumerable duties of a mistress.

In families where there are children and no nurse of any kind is kept, the *mother is the nurse,* and should not attempt to pay and receive formal visits, but content herself with domestic duties until she is in a position to have her afternoons, at least, free. Nothing is more trying to the health and temper than being constantly pulled away from domestic duties by frivolous and inconsiderate visitors.

With the care of her children, their daily walks, and the superintendence of their clothing, the mistress will find but little time for assisting the general servant, who will have, in addition to the work we have mentioned, the preparation of the nursery dinner, and the carrying of water, both hot and cold, to the nurseries, with the cleaning and care of the rooms used by the children.

Spring Cleaning

In spring and autumn more extended cleaning operations go on, and the time for these periodical cleanings is usually

May and October. All white-washing, painting, and general repairs should be done in the spring, and during the cleaning carpets should be taken up, well beaten, mended, and turned so as to bring the worn pieces out of sight. Care must be taken to match the design of the carpet. All ornaments should be carefully washed, cleaned, or relacquered. Chairs and sofas recovered or invested with loose chintz covers. Paper rubbed down with the clean crumb of stale quartern loaves. Ornaments placed in fire-stoves, and white curtains hung up in place of the damask or chintz, which should be well shaken, folded in large folds, with a couple of handfuls of dry bran laid between each fold, and a piece of camphor placed in the drawer or box in which they are kept.

The first thing to be done when beginning a "spring clean," whether in March, April, or May, is to ascertain what pieces of furniture want renovating, and if any require to be taken from home, they should be sent off at once. Then the sweep must be consulted, and ordered to come on the most convenient days. If the family are away, all the rooms can be swept in one day, but if not, the arrangements must be altered by circumstances. To "begin with the top floor and go down" is not a bad rule. Before the sweeps arrival all carpets must come up, and go away or out to be beaten; all ornaments must be removed, pictures taken down, and looking-glasses covered. All furniture should be covered with sheets or with dusting-sheets.

After the sweep's necessary but grimy labours, all traces of his presence must be got rid of, and the room swept *towards* the fireplace, and all dirt taken up, and the stove cleaned. The walls, if paneled, are washed down; if papered, either rubbed down with stale bread or cleaned by passing a clean cloth down them, taking care to remove all cobwebs from corners. In cleaning with bread act as follows:—

First blow off the dust with the bellows. Divide a stale loaf of white bread into eight pieces. Take the crust into your hand, and, beginning at the top of the paper, wipe it *downwards* in the lightest matter with the crumb; do not cross or go upwards; wipe about half a yard at a stroke, and when all the upper part is done, go around again, beginning a little above where you left off. It must be done with great lightness, or the dirt will adhere to the paper, but if properly done the paper looks like new. Then the floor is scrubbed with sand and hot water—*no soap, no soda*—and allowed to dry. The furniture is thoroughly cleansed while the floor is drying.

The furniture should be replaced in position, or changed to suit the altered room, which looks differently with white curtains and a dressed-up fireplace. The fireplace may be concealed by a card-table, with a handsome cover of cloth embroidered with some pretty design. Firegrate adornments are to be avoided by chilly persons, whose health demands that every wet evening, every cold evening, shall see a cheerful fire in the *salon*.

Very pretty modes there are, however, of ornamenting grates and fireplaces. We all know the eternal crinoline, fringed out and adorned with ivy and real or artificial flowers. The blank space filled by looking-glass, with fender of ferns and pot plants in front, is nice but expensive; but the trellis basket-work screen and fender is within the reach of all. The price, to begin with, is moderate, and the trellis is soon covered with creepers, nasturtium, jasmine, clematis. The front or fender may be filled with green moss and cut flowers, or by pots containing growing plants.

Winter curtains must be put away carefully, after hanging out in the air for three or four days if in fine weather, bringing them in at night. On the day you intend to pack them away, beat them lightly with a thin stick, and fold them carefully in as large folds as your store-place will allow, scatter a handful of bran (bone-dry) between each fold, and if placed in a large drawer or closet, add a big lump of camphor.

Lined chintz curtains should be treated in a similar way, but do not require the camphor. The bran cleans both chintz and damask curtains in a wonderful matter, and there is but one thing to remember, that you must carefully shake out the bran when you draw them out again. The nicely washed and mended muslin curtains should hang in their due place, the pictures be replaced in position. And now we turn to the blinds, a vexed subject in many households.

If Venetian blinds are in question, they want simply washing, perhaps repainting, the tapes renovating, not a long business in willing hands; but if the blinds be white holland, on rollers, it is sad work. First, to get the blinds from the rollers, then to wash them and iron them straight, then to replace them, then to find that no one in the house can pull them up straight. Roller-blinds that go up with a gentle spring, and come down with a gentle click-click are best; but if they are not quite clean and new, they should be taken down and made into nice glass-cloths, for which they are well adapted, and new ones placed upon the rollers.

The bedrooms require a few words. The bedding should be taken out of doors, if possible, and well beaten and brushed, the bedstead taken to pieces, whether of wood or of iron, and well washed with hot water and soap. When quite dry the bedding should be replaced, and the summer bed-curtains be arranged with the bed-furniture. An opportunity should be taken of sending all japanned goods out to be repaired, as cans, baths, hot-water cans, etc., All the glass and extra china should be washed or dusted in the china closet, the list gone over, and all missing articles accounted for and replaced as soon as possible.

A few items of housewifery may be jotted down here. Have the pianos tuned as soon as the house-cleaning is over; oil all the door locks, keys, and bolts once every month. Oil all door and window hinges. Have every trifling repair mended at once, and paid for at once; this saves much trouble, and is considerably cheaper than having carpenter's and glazing jobs booked.

Turn out every box, cupboard, and corner in the house-cleaning. Separate all stores required for or likely to be useful in needlework, and keep these in tiny rolls or parcels in a drawer known as the work-drawer. Wash out and fill up inkstands once a week. Few writers like much ink in the inkstand; half an inch deep is quite enough for ordinary writing for a week, and more than enough to spill if there is an accident with the inkstand.

Muslin dresses and petticoats should take the place of the heavier garments, and notable housewives prepare in May their summer costumes for the children and for themselves the little ones look best and are happiest in holland frocks and blouses, or knickerbocker suits of brown holland. Boys of five and six will require four suits a week of these. Little girls are more reasonable, and can be kept in nice order with three suits weekly.

Muslin, holland, or print costumes are nice for morning wear, for ladies' costumes should always be made in accordance with the time they are to be worn. Many ladies in the country do not change their dress until late in the day; the morning costume should be made in dressy style; but if it is discarded before the children's early dinner, it should be as plain as possible, although *always* neat and pretty.

All cloth, merino, and stuff dresses which are worn daily should be hung out for one day in each week in the open air, beaten lightly with a cane, and well brushed, folded, and put away. This cleansing and rest keeps the dress fresh and pleasant, and makes it look better and wear longer than if this little care is neglected.

In the evening various amusements should be allowed in a family—music, cards, reading, games, such as chess, draughts, jacquet, backgammon, etc. A good romp with the little ones is a healthy amusement for everyone who will join in, and most beneficial to the little darlings, who go merrily to "Bedfordshire".

If guests are expected at any time, rooms should be well aired, and everything placed in readiness; chimneys aired by good fires, so as to have no smoke to dishearten the arriving guests, or to blacken the dainty toilet arrangements. In order to allure guests to our table we must give them a good dinner; nay, more, we must have and enjoy the reputation of a good cook, a good cellar, a carefully-appointed table, and quiet, clever waiting. The damask tablecloths must be spotless, the napkins folded in the last mode, flowers arranged on the table with or without the dessert. The glasses should be brilliant, the silver well polished, and plenty of light, either gas, lamp, or, best of all, wax lights.

The waiting should be performed noiselessly. Unless men-servants are thoroughly well drilled, it is better to dispense with their services; at any rate, do not employ anyone from the stable to assist the footman. The aroma arising from the ordinary duties of coachman, groom, or stable-boy is too plainly perceptibly in a dining-room, and is very trying to delicate persons. A neat, nice-looking housemaid is far pleasanter than such "grooms in waiting."

Good housewives will replace all glass and china in fitting order the day following any little party. Fruit should be removed from delicately-painted dessert services as soon as the *convives* assemble in the drawing-room. If there is not time to wash them up at once (by far the best plan), the first opportunity should be taken of doing so, and before going to bed this should be done.

In extinguishing wax candles in chandeliers, candelabra, and piano candle-sticks, care should be taken to avoid disturbing the wax; if blown out, the hand should be placed behind the light to guard the "spirt" of wax from the carpet, but the neatest plan is to have an extinguisher mounted on a long stick, and the lights extinguished one by one with this.

General Servant

Whether the entire workd of a household can be efficiently performed with one servant, is a question very frequently discussed, and one that often gives rise to a very considerable diversity of opinion. The following account of the daily work of a general servant, which we make as accurate and minute as possible, shows how a household can be managed with one servant; we trust that it may prove useful to mistress and maid; more particularly in those cases where, from want of an early training, or from having but recently entered on those duties and responsibilities, the mistress does not possess the knowledge required for ordering her household.

Division of Labour

Is a most important part of household economy. A mistress can assist her servant in her work, and lighten it for her, without having to perform offices uncongenial and distasteful to a woman of education and refinement. In order to explain these relative duties in the most clear and comprehensive matter possible, we give an outline of the servant's work in the order in which it is necessary and most convenient that she should perform it, followed by an outline of the share of the domestic duty which falls most pleasantly and naturally to the mistress, concluding with tried methods of "the best mode of doing things."

Early rising is a most essential point; therefore, as a rule, six, summer and winter, is the hour at which to rise. The morning work, with fires and extra boot-cleaning, is heavier in winter than in summer; therefore at that season the maid can less afford to lie late in bed.

On coming downstairs she should open all the shutters, and, if the weather be fine, the windows of all the lower rooms. She should then go to the kitchen, and having cleared out the remains of the fire of the night before, and brushed up, blacked, and brightened the range, she should proceed—

Sweep the Breakfast-room

Having laid down a coarse cloth over the carpet in front of the fireplace, she will first clear away all the cinders and ashes from the grate, putting them in the cinder-pail. This is a japanned tin pail, with a wire sifter inside and a closely fitting top. In this the cinders are sifted, and reserved for use in the kitchen or for the copper-fire, the ashes alone being thrown away. She will then blacklead the grate, first laying on the blacklead with a soft brush, then brushing it vigorously with a hard one, finishing it off with a polishing brush.

No blacklead is to be put upon any portions of the grate that may be of polished steel; these should be rubbed with a clean dry leather and putty powder. If any spots of rust appear, a paste made of fresh lime and oil should at once be applied, and renewed until it has disappeared; the fire-irons are to be cleaned in the same way if bright, and then rubbed with the leather; all the bright-steel portions of the fender should be rubbed with the leather; emery-paper must on no account be used to bright steel.

She will then light the fire. Fire-lighting, however simple, is an operation requiring some skill. A fire is readily made by laying a few cinders at the bottom in open order; over this a few pieces of paper, and over that again eight or ten pieces of dry wood; over the wood, a course of moderate-sized pieces of coal, taking care to leave hollow spaces between for air at the centre, and taking care to lay the whole well back in the grate, so that the smoke may go up the chimney and not into the room. This done, fire the paper with a match from below, and, if properly laid, it will soon burn up; the stream of flame from the wood and paper soon communicating to the coals and cinders, provided there is plenty of air at the centre.

A new method of lighting a fire is sometimes practiced with advantage, the fire lighting from the top and burning down, in place of being lighted and burning up from below. This is arranged by laying the coals at the bottom, mixed with a few good-sized cinders, and the wood at the top, with another layer of coals and some paper over it; the paper is lighted in the usual way, and soon burns down to a good fire, with some economy of fuel, it is said.

That being done, she will clean the hearthstone, bringing up for the purpose a small pail of hot water, a house-flannel, and a piece of hearthstone. Having well washed the hearthstone, she will whiten it by rubbing it well with the hearthstone; but in doing this she must be very careful to let none of the water touch the grate, fender, or fire-irons. Then, having removed all her brushes and boxes, the dust-pan, pail, house-flannel, and stone, and having shut the parlour-door, she will sweep the hall, using for it the house-sweeping brush, and not the carpet-broom. She will also sweep the halldoor-steps, and, taking out the door-mats, beat and shake them well.

Then she will return to the breakfast-room, where the dust will be by this time settled, and dust it all carefully. In doing this, she will be particular not to omit dusting the legs of the various pieces of furniture, and lifting and dusting under as well as round all the small articles on chimneypiece, sideboard, side-table, and bookshelves, also the window-ledges and sills.

To Clean Boots

She should then clean any boots unavoidably left since the night before; after which, the last of the morning's "dirty work" being done, the servant goes upstairs and knocks at the different bedroom doors to "call" the family, supplying those who require it with warm water, which—not to empty her kettle—she should draw from the boiler, where, by this time, it will be quite warm enough, except for shaving-water, which must be boiling and taken from the kettle. She should then go to her own room, wash her face and hands, brush her hair, and put on a clean cap and apron.

To Lay the Breakfast-table

Servants should collect on her tray, placing them carefully, the large plates one over another, and the small plates on them; the four saucers one over another, and two of the cups one within the other on them, the other two cups one within the other in the slop-basin; the tablecloths and napkins are usually kept in the sideboard drawer.

Having spread the cloth carefully, she should lay at each person's place a large and small knife, a fork, and a large and small plate; the knives are to be at the right hand side of the large plates and close to them, the forks at the left and close too, the small egg-plates next to the forks; the cups and saucers should the ranged together before the mistress's place, the teapot, or coffee-urn, stand behind them, and the slop-basin next to it, the milk-jug and sugar-basin on the other side; the small carving-knife and fork should be put with his own knife and fork at the master's place, and a mat before it for the hot dish, the tablespoon, placed lengthwise, in front of that; the teaspoons should be put each in one of the saucers, the egg-spoons each on one of the small plates, and the napkins each on one of the large plates; the cruet-stand in the centre of the table, one of the salt-cellars at the right hand top corner, the other at the right hand bottom corner of the table; the dessert-spoon placed on the plate with the marmalade, which will be taken from the cellaret; the butter-knife laid close to the butter-dish, the bread-knife in the bread-platter, the large carving-knife and fork on the sideboard.

This being done, she will bring up the cold meat, having first put it on a clean dish, and place it on the sideboard; bring up the bread in the bread-basket or on the bread-platter, which should be clean and white, and place it at the side of the table and the butter in the butter-dish, where the mistress will put the sugar-basin when she takes it from the cellaret. Should there be a portion of a loaf of bread cut the day before, that should be brought up; but unless it be more than half a loaf, an entire one should be brought up also. About a quarter of a pound of butter will be sufficient, and half a pint of milk.

Get the Breakfast Ready

The kettle being boiling, she will move it a little to be side—still keeping it boiling—to make room for the pan or gridiron. Having put down the rashers of bacon, or whatever other meat is to be cooked for breakfast, and put a dish and four plates into the oven to warm, she may, while attending to the meat, make, if any of the family require it, two or three rounds of thin toast, which, as soon as each one is finished, should be placed in the toast-rack. The meat being cooked, it should be put on the hot dish, and covered close to keep warm.

When the family have finished breakfast, she should first clear away the breakfast things, then take up the crumbs in the dustpan, arrange the chairs in their places, and sweep up the hearth. Where but one servant is kept, and in a town house, it is better immediately after breakfast to attend to *downstair* work, rather than go to make up the bedrooms. For, as between nine and ten o'clock is the usual hour for tradespeople to call, the continued running up and down stairs to attend to them, if she be engaged in the upper part of the house, besides being a severe tax upon her strength, greatly retards a servant in work. The unavoidable delays, too, which it occasions in attending to them, is a considerable trial to the patience of the butcher and greengrocer, who are also trying to get through *their* morning's work as quickly as possible. After breakfast, therefore, the first thing for the general servant to do is to—

Wash up the Breakfast Things

When all the things are done they should be put instantly by, the plates and dishes in their appointed places on the dresser, the china cups and saucers in the cupboard, the knives in the knife-basket, the silver in the plate-basket, and at once taken up to the dining-room, and placed in the cellaret, and locked in.

The servant should then wash down the kitchen-table, empty, wipe out, and put aside the pail, hang up the towels to try, clean and put aside the egg-saucepan and frying-pan; arrange the kitchen fire, sweep up the hearth, and generally tidy up the kitchen for her mistress's inspection.

To Arrange the Bedroom

The first thing to be done in the rooms is to empty the slops, and for this she should take with her the slop-pail, a jug of boiling water, and two slop-cloths. Then dust the room thoroughly, lifting all the things from the dressing-table and chimney-piece and wiping each, dusting the looking-glass back and front, and removing, by rubbing, any spots that may appear on the plate. She should also dust the top and front of the chest of drawers, the front of the wardrobe, the sills and ledges of the windows and the door, she should then fill the water-jugs with soft and the bottles with clean cold water.

Having completely finished one room, she should proceed to the next, and so through them all; and when all are done, she should take downstairs all the candlesticks and hot-water jugs. Besides this ordinary cleaning, each bedroom in the house should get a thorough cleaning once a week; and they should be taken in regular rotation with the other work. Thus the following is a good division:—

To Clean Marble

Mix with ¼ pint of soap-lees, ½ gill of turpentine, sufficient pipe-clay and bullocks' gall to make the whole into a rather thick paste. Apply it to the marble with a soft brush, and after a day or two, when quite dry, rub it off with a soft rag. Apply this a second or third time, till the marble is quite clean.

Another Method—Take two parts of soda, one of pumice-stone, and one of finely-powdered chalk. Sift these through a fine sieve, and mix them into a paste with water. Rub this well over the marble, and the stains will be removed: then wash it with soap and water, and a beautiful bright polish will be produced.

She will then wash with soap and *warm* water if it be summer, but *cold* water if it be frosty winter weather, the window-panes, as much as she can get at without going outside. The warm soap and water should be applied first briskly with the flannel; the glass should then be rinsed down with cold water, and dried and polished off afterwards with clean, dry cloths. For the rinsing, a sponge will be found very useful. The window-sills, if dirty, should also be washed, but, like the door, gently, for fear of injuring the paint.

To Clean Windows

With a clean washleather, kept for the purpose alone, wash down the windows with clean cold water, moving the leather one way only (downwards); rinse in clean water, and repeat with the rung-out leather. Wash all the windows in this way both inside and out, and leave them to dry.

Scour the Bedroom

For this, if the room be scoured regularly once a fortnight, she will require nothing more than plenty of clean cold soft water, a good scrubbing-brush, and a house-flannel. Having scrubbed well with the brush, and plenty of water, a portion as far as her arm will reach, she should dry it off with the flannel before moving to do another portion, and she must be careful not to omit scrubbing equally all the floor, else it will have a patchy appearance afterwards, some portions being whiter than others. She should also empty her pail and refill it with clean water very frequently.

Take up the Luncheon

The things required for this will depend upon the nature

of the meal. If tea or coffee is used, cups and saucers must be taken up. Cold meat must be placed on a clean dish, and plates, besides the small breakfast-plates, supplied for it. Also large knives and forks, and a carving knife and fork, tumblers and wine-glasses, and a sufficient number of articles, whatever be the kind used, must be provided for the number of people as at breakfast: if four people, four of everything. The table will be laid the same as at breakfast, only that, if there are but one or two ladies for luncheon, it will be sufficient to lay the cloth over half the table only.

While the family are at luncheon she should take her own dinner, then remove and wash up the things. After this she should take out a sufficient supply of coals for the rest of the day; when, all dirty work being over, she should go up and dress herself for the afternoon. From this time (about two o'clock) until four she may occupy herself with starching, sprinkling, and folding, or ironing, any things of her own or her mistress's that go in the week's home wash, which she can do, and keep herself clean and tidy at the same time to attend the hall-door during this the usual visiting hour.

Get the Dinner Ready

However, if a large joint has to be roasted, she would have to began her preparations earlier. For example, an 8-lb. leg of mutton would take from a quarter before four; but if the dinner were to consist of cold meat, fried fish, and soup, perhaps made the day before, if she set to work at half-past four she would have ample time for all preparations. This part of a servant's business, however, varies so much with each day's dinner, that it is impossible to lay down any exact rule to be precisely followed each day; but when a servant knows from experience the length of time it will take her to prepare a number of dishes of certain kinds, she should always commence sufficiently early to allow herself that length of time, and not try and cheat herself into the belief that she can do it equally well in half. If a shoulder of mutton weighing 7 lb., gravy soup, an apple-tart, mashed turnips and potatoes are ordered for dinner at 4 o'clock, she should put down the joint, then she should make the tart (putting it in a cool place afterwards), then lay the cloth for dinner, then put in the turnips, then the potatoes, then put the tart in the oven.

While the turnips and potatoes are boiling she should clear the soup, and add the vegetables thereto. At a quarter to six she should take up the turnips, and if quite tender, mash them, adding the butter and pepper and salt; put them back in the saucepan, and place it at the side of the fire to keep warm. The gravy for the mutton should then be prepared. At six precisely the soup should be served, and, having handed round the potatoes, the servant should return to the kitchen and dish the mutton and vegetables, which she will get done just by the time the family are ready for them.

To Lay the Dinner Table

Everything should be as clean as possible. The bread-plates free from crumbs, the butter-dish unsmeared with butter, the salt-cellars bright and filled with fine salt, the cruet-stand quite bright and clean, the mustard-pot half filled with fresh mustard, the vinegar-bottle filled with vinegar, and the other bottles with whatever sauces may be used. If dessert and wine be taken, the dessert will be placed down the middle of the table, in which case the cruet-stand will be put on the sideboard, and a vase of flowers substituted for it on the table. The wine will be placed at the corners of table, inside the salt-cellars and table-spoons; if there are but two decanters one will be placed at the right hand top corner and one at the right hand bottom corner.

When dessert and wine are used, four dessert plates and four dessert knives will have to be brought up and placed on the sideboard. Four additional table-spoons will also have to be put on the table at the other corners. Each person must have as many glasses as there are different kinds of wines. If only sherry and claret, a sherry and claret glass to each person; if sherry, claret, and port, a sherry glass, claret glass, and port glass to each person.

2

Organisation of Housekeeping Management

Most hotels and motels are commercial properties that cater mainly to business people, tourists, and other travelers who need accommodations for a brief stay. Commercial hotels and motels usually are located in cities or suburban areas and operate year round. Larger properties offer a variety of services for their guests, including coffee shops, restaurants, and cocktail lounges with live entertainment. Some even provide gift shops, newsstands, barber and beauty shops, laundry and valet services, theater and airline counters, swimming pools, and fitness centers and health spas. Larger hotels and motels often have banquet rooms, exhibit halls, and spacious ballrooms to accommodate conventions, business meetings, wedding receptions, and other social gatherings. Conventions and business meetings are major sources of revenue for these hotels and motels.

Some commercial hotels are known as conference hotels—fully self-contained entities specifically designed for meetings. They provide physical and recreational facilities for meetings, in addition to state-of-the-art audiovisual and technical equipment. Resort hotels and motels offer luxurious surroundings with a variety of recreational facilities such as swimming pools, golf courses, tennis courts, gamerooms, and health spas, as well as planned social activities and entertainment. Resorts are located primarily in vacation destinations near mountains, the seashore, or other attractions. As a result, the business of many resorts fluctuates with the season.

Some resort hotels and motels provide additional convention and conference facilities to encourage customers to combine business with pleasure. During their off season, these establishments solicit conventions, sales meetings, and incentive tours to fill their otherwise empty rooms. Residential hotels provide living quarters for permanent and semipermanent residents. They combine the comfort of apartment living with the convenience of hotel services. Many have dining rooms and restaurants that also are open to the general public.

Extended-stay hotels combine features of a resort and a residential hotel. Typically, guests use these hotels for a minimum of 5 consecutive nights. These facilities usually provide rooms with fully equipped kitchens, entertainment systems, ironing boards and irons, office spaces with computer and telephone lines, access to fitness centers, and other amenities. Casino hotels generally offer a full range of services and amenities and may also contain conference and convention facilities.

In addition to hotels and motels, bed-and-breakfast inns, recreational vehicle (RV) parks, campgrounds, and rooming and boarding houses provide lodging for overnight guests. Bed-and-breakfast inns provide short-term lodging in private homes or small buildings converted for this purpose and are characterised by highly personalised service and inclusion of a full breakfast in the room rate. RV parks and recreational camps cater to people who enjoy recreational camping at moderate prices. Some parks and campgrounds provide service stations, general stores, shower and toilet facilities, and coin-operated laundries.

While some are designed for overnight travelers only, others are for vacationers who stay longer. Some camps provide accommodations, such as cabins and fixed campsites, and other amenities, such as food services, recreational facilities and equipment, and organised recreational activities. Examples of these overnight camps include, children's camps, family vacation camps, hunting and fishing camps, and outdoor adventure retreats that offer trail riding, white-water rafting, hiking, and similar activities. Other short-term lodging facilities in this industry include guesthouses, or small cottages located on the same property as a main residence, and youth hostels—dormitory-style hotels with few frills, occupied mainly by students traveling on low budgets. Also included are rooming and boarding houses, such as fraternity houses, sorority houses, off-campus dormitories, and workers' camps.

In recent years, hotels, motels, camps, and recreational and RV parks affiliated with national chains have been growing rapidly. To the traveler, familiar chain establishments represent dependability and quality at predictable rates. National corporations own many chains, although several others are independently owned but affiliated with a chain through a franchise agreement. Increases in competition and in the sophistication of travelers have induced the chains to provide lodging to serve a variety of customer budgets and accommodation preferences.

In general, these lodging places may be grouped into properties that offer luxury, all-suite, moderately priced, and economy accommodations. The numbers of limited-service or economy chain properties—economy lodging without lobbies, restaurants, lounges, and meeting rooms—have been growing. These properties are not as costly to build and operate. They appeal to budget-conscious family vacationers and travelers who are willing to sacrifice amenities for lower room prices.

While economy chains have become more prevalent, the movement in the hotel and lodging industry is towards more extended-stay properties. In addition to fully equipped kitchenettes and laundry services, the extended-stay market offers guest amenities such as in-room access to the Internet and grocery shopping. This segment of the hotels and other accommodations industry has eliminated traditional hotel lobbies and 24-hour personnel, and housekeeping is usually done only about once a week. This helps to keep costs to a minimum. All-suite facilities, especially popular with business travelers, offer a living room and a bedroom.

LODGING

Lodging facilities that were used for economic purposes were built along transportation routes where travelling parties found it convenient to make rest stops en route to their destinations. In Marco Polo's time, rest areas were strategically placed at a distance of a day's ride by caravan. Polo was able to travel from Venice to the Mongol Empire of Kublai Khan in Central Asia by making scheduled stops along the way, where food and safe shelter were available. Chaucer's Canterbury Tales, written around 1390 in England, contains lively descriptions of inn-keeping practices of the time. In Don Quixote, many of Cervantes' ideals are put into practice at an inn in La Mancha, Spain. What we know today as inns had their origin in England some centuries ago, the term meaning "a public house that provides lodging for travellers and others." These taverns with rooms for rent were usually located along highways to provide a convenient overnight stay for those travelling by coach.

The introduction of railways in the nineteenth century created the need for a large number of these hostelries along the numerous lines that crisscrossed the country. Today, the term inn implies a small hotel, although properties called "inns" often contain a large number of rooms; for example the Holiday Inn Crowne Plaza in New Orleans has 439 guestrooms. The term hotel derives from the French hostel. The modern French word hotel suggests "a more or less commodious establishment with up-to-date appointments," though this was not necessarily true one hundred years ago.

Today, the term hotel defines a lodging establishment offering accommodation, food and beverage, and amenities to guests. The New Orleans' Windsor Court Hotel, which consumers have rated as one of the best hotels in the United States, advertises meeting facilities, outdoor pool, health club, ballrooms, concierge services, five-diamond dining room, chamber music, and 24-hour suite service. Nightly rates at the Windsor Court range from $320 for regular guestrooms to $990 for two-bedroom suites. The first spas were operated in Europe and consisted of resorts located by mineral springs, which were believed to have curative powers. Today, spas offer a wide array of health-related services ranging from curative massage and mud baths to weightloss programmes.

Lodging properties can be independently owned, owned by a multi-unit chain, franchised, or managed by a management company. Properties that are independently owned are not affiliated with any multiple -property entity and are usually managed by their owners. This type of property still represents the largest segment of the lodging industry. A typical in dependently owned establishment is small in size and is located in a relatively small community. There are advantages and disadvantages to independent operation: on the positive side, independent lodging establishments can provide guests with unique, personalised service while saving royalty and management fees that otherwise would have to be paid to franchisors and/or management companies.

On the negative side, such properties may not have name recognition to travellers, they lack collective advertising power, and they are unable to benefit from a national/international reservation system. Often, independently owned and managed properties join reservation referral systems and marketing associations, such as Best Western International, Leading Hotels and Resorts, or Utell International. Chain properties operate under the direct control of the chain's headquarters. Establishments belonging to the same chain display the same logo and offer identical services by category. For instance, a Hilton four-star hotel must provide similar service and amenities whether it is located in Florida or in Oregon. This assures guests of consistency in price, room layout, menus, sports facilities, and so on.

Lodging properties can also be categorised by service. Economy or budget properties focus on meeting the basic needs of the travelling public-that is, clean, comfortable rooms that are not expensive. The market segments typically attracted to economy properties are guests travelling with children, bus tours, and budget-minded retirees. Many of these properties do not offer food and beverage services except for breakfast, although they all feature TV and some have a swimming pool, whirlpool, and tennis courts. Mid-market properties offer all the amenities expected in a "home -away-from -home setting."

Restaurants, coffee shops, bars, luggage service, meeting rooms, health club, and room service are generally offered in such properties. The quality of bed linen, towels, room furniture, lobby decor, and customer service must be good or very good. Travellers who frequent properties of this type are business people, individual tourists, conventioneers, and guests wishing to receive a guaranteed level of excellent service. Often, mid-market properties feature suites that consist of a bedroom, adjacent living room, and a kitchenette with refrigerator. Suites are very appealing to families with children or to two couples travelling together.

Luxury properties offer world-class service, which includes any type of convenience that would be expected by any traveller in any country in the world. Committed to the ultimate in hospitality, luxury properties may feature extravagant amenities like Godiva or other imported chocolates, speciality toiletry items, slippers, silk robes, and special services like executive floors, concierge, foreign language translators, nanny, and private secretary. The American Automobile Association (AAA) is the most common rater of lodging establishments in the United States. As a service to its members, this organisation provides travel guides that are updated annually describing the properties and evaluating their services.

The ratings are determined by field inspectors who base their decisions on thorough evaluations of the properties' design, decor, fittings, comfort, and of their levels of service, cleanliness and upkeep. In general, AAA awards three diamonds to economy establishments while mid-market properties are assigned four diamonds. Invariably, luxury hotels and resorts receive a rating of five diamonds.

The housekeeping categories used by the housekeeping department usually include: housekeeping salaries and wages, payroll taxes and benefits, and other expenses. Salaries and wages include those of the entire housekeeping department; payroll taxes and benefits include the operator's share of additional costs related to payroll; the category of other expenses encompasses any other cost incurred by the housekeeping department that is not payroll-related. The buying function in lodging chains is often centralised. Items like soap, linen, mattresses, pillows, furniture, and fixtures are procured by the company's purchasing department and shipped to the different units on request.

Purchasing in large independent properties is done by the purchasing agent, who is a specialised buyer in charge of procuring products for all departments in the property. Smaller properties often allow the department heads to purchase goods for their respective areas of responsibility. In any case, it should be the job of the executive housekeeper to always pretest and approve all items used in the housekeeping department and decide the quantities and the specifications of the products to be bought. It should not be the job of the purchasing agent, or any other person for that matter, to purchase material and supplies without the consent of the executive housekeeper. It is also important to solicit the input of janitors, section housekeepers, housepersons, and laundry personnel on the appropriate characteristics of the items that in the end are to be used by them.

All merchandise purchased should have precise specifications, which are descriptions of the products' quality and factors that should reflect precisely the performance needs for each particular institution. Specifications should be stated clearly, giving the information needed to assure proper identification. For instance, a luxury resort does probably require the best bed linen money can buy, while a small, inexpensive motel may just need bed linen of fair quality. Before buying a product, prices should be obtained from at least three different vendors. Product price and vendor dependability and service should be reviewed once or twice every three months. Purchasing decisions should be made based not only on price but on quality, suitability, and storage availability as well.

The executive housekeeper must control the function of purchasing by defining clearly what is to be procured, who will be in charge of the buying, what specifications are to be considered, and what quantities will be needed. The person in charge of purchasing must consistently provide the needed quantities of products in housekeeping inventories. Although in some cases purchasing is done by the corporate office or by the property's purchasing agent, the executive housekeeper is ultimately responsible for the cost and results of what is purchased.

For some products, linen for instance, pars need to be established; for others, for example soaps and paper products, maximum and minimum quantities are set up. Pars can be defined as the number of required on-hand items to perform housekeeping operations. In the case of linens, for instance, the optimum number of pars is 4. This means that ideally the property should have on hand one set of sheets and pillowcases set up in the guestroom beds at any given time, another set being laundered, an additional set ready to go in floor closets and room attendant carts, and one final set on reserve. For guest and cleaning supplies, the maximum quantity is the greatest number of units that should be in stock at any given time, while the minimum quantity refers to the fewest number of units.

For example, the maximum and minimum number of cases of soap could be 35 and 25 respectively. That means that if at any given time the soap inventory is above 35, the product is overstocked. On the other hand, if the number of cases falls below 25, additional supplies must be ordered. This system eliminates the risk of overstocking or of running out of products. The receiving function of goods ordered must also be controlled. Unless adequate inspection and receiving procedures are used, the best purchasing system may fail because it is at this point that determination must be made of whether or not the products meet the specifications and quantities of the order previously placed.

Failing to inspect the merchandise adequately may result in higher costs, lower quality, theft, and fraud. On receiving a shipment, the goods should be compared with those listed on the receiving sheet or purchase order to verify the correctness of the delivery. If the goods meet the prearranged requirements, they are accepted by signing the invoice or delivery memo. If the products do not meet inspection requirements, they should be refused and a notation indicating the reasons for refusing the delivery made. The function of storing merchandise must also be controlled adequately. Access to storerooms must be limited to authorised personnel only. The storeroom should be locked off -hours and a record should be kept of the person entering it and of the merchandise taken. Valuable items like towels and some guest supplies should be stored in an area that remains locked at all times.

The storage area should be designed to hold the specific products stored in it; bottom shelving levels should be at least 10 inches off the floor to ensure adequate ventilation and to allow for cleaning underneath. A rotation system should be established by which oldest stock is placed in front and issued first. In large properties, housekeeping items may be stored in the main storeroom. In this case, the housekeeping department will need to fill a requisition form to request products.

Floor closet storage should also be locked at all times and access limited to the section housekeepers, housepersons, or supervisors in charge of the area. To account for the cost of housekeeping operating assets used, physical inventories are conducted regularly, in most cases monthly. Linens, uniforms, and cleaning and guest supplies inventories are taken by counting all items on hand and listing them on a physical inventory form. Laundry chemicals may be included in the cleaning supplies category or counted separately for better control. The purpose of taking physical inventories is to find out what amount of items for each category is on hand and to work out its current market value.

Physical inventories are difficult to conduct as all items that need to be accounted for must be counted one by one. In the case of linens, for instance, linens are found in guestrooms, laundry room, linen room, floor closets, room attendant carts, etc. To keep tight control on valuable items, for example imported chocolates for special guests, a perpetual inventory system may be implemented. Executive housekeepers must administer and maintain their proprieties' fixed assets classified as Furniture, Fixtures and Equipment (FF&E), Software, and Department Equipment. Although new establishments are usually handed over to the management team equipped with allitems needed for operation, the executive housekeeper is directly involved in the replacement, refurbishing, and upkeep of most fixed asset items in the property. For this reason, executive housekeepers must have appropriate knowledge of the assets that are under their control.

Regardless of their type of service, lodging properties must maintain interior design consistency standards throughout the building. Whether a property has been classified as economy, mid-market, or luxury, its guestroom and public area design, colour patterns, fabric and upholstery quality, and overall appearance must befit the category they represent. Doing piecemeal refurbishing or renovating must always be avoided. Colours, for instance, must be complementary. In general, blue is a complement of orange, green of red, and yellow of violet. Using several light tints and shades of the same colour makes rooms seem larger, while full-intensity hues tend to make the room seem compact. Adjoining walls should be painted the same colour to provide a sense of continuity.

Executive housekeepers are generally responsible for the refurbishing and upkeep of the furniture in guestroom, public, and employee areas. Furniture should be solidly built, easy to maintain, functional, and attractive. It is not advisable to purchase pieces of furniture directly from a catalogue; instead, the executive housekeeper should carefully examine samples to ensure that the products have been built to withstand repeated rough use. All furniture tops should be plastic-laminated or finished with water-repellent polyurethane to avoid scratches, rings, and stains caused by abusive treatment and spilled liquids.

Desk chairs should have padded backs to provide comfort to guests and prevent wood from hitting desktops. Furniture dotted with glides or casters will prevent carpet damage when pushed or pulled around the room. Luggage racks are better if built-in and fitted with wall-protecting panels, as there is a greater likelihood that the luggage will bump against and deteriorate walls when detached racks are used. Desks should be large enough to accommodate a desktop computer and a fax machine.

TV/VCR units should be an actual piece of furniture, rather than simply a conventional metal stand, and should be fitted with 180-degree swivels so that guests can see the screen from anywhere in the room. Case furniture such as chests of drawers, credensas, armoires, desks, and bureaus also should be purchased with durability in mind. Drawers should be equipped with nylon ball bearings and slide glides so that they don't jam when opening and closing. In general, guestrooms should provide a warm residential look; for instance, love seats and armchairs can replace the standard chairs so often found in hotel rooms. Upholstery fibers may be natural, synthetic, or plastic.

Natural fabrics, such as cotton, linen, silk, and wool, are rich looking and long wearing but expensive and delicate to maintain because they stain easily. Synthetic fibers are less expensive and easy to clean but they are less elegant and more likely to generate static electricity. Often, upholstered materials are a blend of natural and synthetic fabrics. The greatest advantage of upholstery plastic materials such as vinyl is that they can be easily cleaned by just wiping with a soapy cloth; however, they generally have a duller appearance than natural or blended materials.

Upholstery fabrics should be strong enough to withstand repeated shampooing. Treating fabrics With soil-retardant sprays can decrease the need for dry-cleaning the material. It is also important that upholstery fabrics be treated with flame-retardant finishes. Before putting upholstered furniture fabrics into use, they should be pretested to ascertain the best way to clean the pieces without causing shrinkage or discoloration. Some fabrics can be cleaned with solvent, others can be cleaned with water and detergent, and some only allow for vacuuming. In general, synthetic fabrics such as nylon and plastics such as vinyl are the most stain-resistant and easy-to-clean upholstery materials. Beds are the central attraction in guestrooms and often a big selling point for travellers when choosing a lodging property. When asked to pay an average of $70.00 per night per room, guests expect to receive a clean, well-maintained sleeping area and a comfortable bed.

In commercial operations, beds consist of a frame to support the springs and mattresses and unattached headboards. Bed frames usually consist of metal bars with legs attached to each corner or of a metal or wood platform. The main advantage of platform frames is that room attendants don't have to vacuum underneath the box frame, thus saving time when cleaning the room. Headboards are mounted on the wall and should match the general design of the room's furniture. It is important to know the composition of the bed structure of each property in order to figure out the maximum member of people that the property can house.

Knowing the different types of beds and how many guests can stay in the rooms will help executive housekeepers plan for bed and bathroom linen and supplies. Another type of sleeping equipment is the mobile bed. Families on vacation and travelling high school or college groups often require additional sleeping accommodations in guestrooms. The rollaway, or bed on wheels, consists of a folding frame with an attached bed spring body. The mattress in rollaways must be made of latex foam or have very light, flexible innersprings so that they too can fold with the frame. Because rollaways are unable to provide a comfortable surface to hold the weight of an adult person, they should be recommended only for children or young people to avoid legitimate complaints about the property's not providing adequate accommodation.

Cribs are also essential to have in order to accommodate infants or young children. While cribs should be collapsible to save storage space, their extension mechanisms should be kept in good working order to prevent the crib from collapsing when being used. Dual-purpose sleeping equipment is common in guestrooms. These pieces of furniture provide both seating space and extra sleeping capacity, eliminating the need to roll in a mobile bed on short notice. Sofas, couches, chair-beds, and in-wall beds are the most common dual-purpose pieces of furniture found in lodging properties. Sofas, couches and chair-beds convert into beds by removing the cushions and pulling out the folding frame and mattress or by dropping the back to the level of the seat. In-wall beds, also called Murphy beds, are concealed in the wall behind a panel, giving the room the appearance of a studio or parlour rather than a bedroom.

Surveys of favourite guest amenities conducted regularly by hospitality magazines consistently show that guests put comfortable mattresses at the top of the list, second only to cleanliness. Most mattresses used in lodging operations are of the innerspring type; they have metal coils that support the weight of the sleepers while conforming to their body contours. The strength and number of coils determine the mattress firmness, which may range from medium to super firm. Heavy-gauge steel wire coils are best, allowing for weights to flex down a specific area without disturbing the space surrounding the pressure points. This allows for two persons of different weights to lie side by side and each get different levels of buoyancy.

The firmness of the mattress is determined by the gauge of steel used, the number of turns of each coil, and the way the coils are attached to the mattress frame. Preferably, the springs should be encased in fabric pockets to provide independent coil action, rather than being attached to each other with wire or hooks. Good mattresses have sufficient padding to cushion the springs beneath and provide a smooth surface. The padding should be nonallergenic and comply with the government flame-spread regulation, which states that a lighted cigarette should not be able to ignite the insulation.

Water-filled mattresses (waterbeds) became quite popular with the public when they were first used in the 1960s, but they soon proved to be inconvenient with lodging operators because they often leaked and because the water had to be heated, which became costly. Although today's waterbeds are efficiently built with individually filled cells that do not need to be heated because of an insulating foam layer, there doesn't seem to be a great demand for them from lodging guests. Lodging properties, however, should have a few waterbeds to fulfil the request of interested travellers. Guestrooms and lodging property lobbies are also furnished with accessories such as mirrors, decorations, pictures, and lights, to complement the furniture.

For instance, strategically placed mirrors can give small rooms an illusion of depth; serene motifs in paintings will provide a feeling of tranquillity; triple magnification make-up mirrors and wall-mounted hair dryers in bathrooms are a welcome amenity; a well-stocked mahogany bookcase in the lobby will provide a homey feeling to guests who enjoy reading. Beautiful carpeting can enhance the appearance of lodging properties and make a lasting impression on guests. On the other hand, discoloured, worn, or dirty carpets are usually sources of guest complaints. The first step in selecting the right carpet is to match its colour, texture, and pattern with the design of the area where it is to be installed.

Then, other factors need to be considered, such as determining the anticipated level of wear and tear caused by the intensity of traffic, the location of the carpet, and the budget allocated for it. When heavy traffic is expected, carpets should feature strong resistance to abrasion, as well as texture retention and anti-soiling and staining characteristics. The location of the carpet should determine specifications such as enhanced colourfastness, antimicrobial protection, resistance to snags, and resilience under rolling loads.

Besides durability and stain resistance, carpets in lodging properties should be capable of withstanding repeated cleaning treatment. Before purchasing carpet, be sure you fully understand the warranty coverage offered by the manufacturer or installer. Warranties for commercial carpets should include protection for wear and tear, colourfastness (fading from sunlight and atmospheric contaminants), tuft bind deterioration, static charges, backing strength, ravelling of seams and edges, and any other manufacturing defects.

Executive housekeepers should have sufficient knowledge of carpet construction to ensure that the right carpet is selected for each area in the property. There are three main elements in the composition of carpets: the pile, or face; the backing, or material to which the pile is secured; and the padding, or cushion on which the carpet rests. Most commercial carpets are tufted, that is, the yam is threaded through the backing material to form loops. The backing material usually is woven jute or polypropylene with a layer of adhesive latex extended over the material to anchor the tufts. Knitted carpets are made by interlacing together the pile yam and the backing.

The process of embedding the pile fibers electrostatically into a layer of adhesive material applied to the backing is called flocking. Weaving is the old-fashioned way of making carpets using conventional looms. The yarns are interlaced together to form the pile and the backing. As with linen, the yarns woven lengthwise are called the warp and the yarns going across are the wefts. The process of making carpets by compacting the fibers and the backing by mechanically punching them together is called needle punching. Improper lighting in rooms may discourage guests from staying in a particular establishment.

Guests, particularly business travellers, expect to find adequate lighting to be able to work over flat surfaces such as tables and desks, or to read in bed or sitting on a couch or armchair. Lights of adjustable intensity should be placed strategically so that guests can arrange their preferences to suit their needs; for example, subdued lighting for relaxation or bright lighting for working or entertaining friends. Having three-way lamps or lights activated by rheostats give guests the option to set the mood of the room to their liking. Floor lamps are not recommended in guestrooms because they can be easily knocked over and they create tripping hazards. Desk lamps should have the on-off switches at the base to reduce the risk of guests burning their fingers on the light bulb or upsetting the shade's balance when reaching around to locate the switch.

One advantage of fluorescent lights is that they use less energy and last longer than regular bulbs. In all cases, sufficient wattage must be provided in lamps that guests will use for reading or working purposes. Long gone are the days when hoteliers could sell rooms equipped with a minimum of basic features. Today's business traveller is putting a new spin on the concept of guestroom equipment. Lodging chains that cater to corporate clientele offer in-room or satellite office support services including computers and fax and copy machines. Guestrooms are often equipped with multi-line telephones complete with voice mail and PC compatibility; some hotels even provide cellular phones and 24-hour access to translators and information in other languages.

Refrigerators and microwave ovens are quite common in suite hotels, and coffee-makers, together with selections of coffee and tea blends, are now available in the rooms of most properties. Wide-screen television sets and high-quality clock radios are a must in four- and five-diamond properties, as are in-room safes. In-room strongboxes are seen as a last-ditch defence for the guests' personal belongings, including items as large as lap-top computers. The locking systems of in-room safes range from ordinary keys to programmable push-buttons, magnetic-lock devices, and the guest's credit card. Some microprocessor safes automatically lock for 30 minutes after four false attempts to open them. Besides being a great convenience for guests who don't want to line up for safety deposit boxes, in-room safes are effective against thieves and even employees who may use stolen keys to burglarize rooms.

Valuables can be stored by guests themselves and remain secure during trips to the pool, jogging around the block, or going out to dinner. Some safes have built-in memory, which enables the front office personnel to read the date and time of the most recent safe openings and closings. This can provide convincing evidence in case of a loss claim against the property. Some up-scale lodging properties, particularly resorts and first class hotels, offer minibars in their guestrooms and suites.

Stocked with beverages and snacks, minibars can be profitable because guests are often tempted to have a last drink before going to bed or first thing in the morning. Fully automated minibars can electronically sense when an item is removed, sending the corresponding charge to the guest's room account. Non-automated units must rely on the honesty of the guest to notify the front desk just before checking out if goods have been consumed. Depreciable fixed assets that are not furniture or equipment, such as bedspreads, mattress covers, blankets, pillows, and window coverings may be categorised under the classification of software.

As with mattresses, bedspreads should be purchased with the qualities of durability, comfort, maintenance, and fire safety in mind. Bedspreads are an important component in the decor of guestrooms and should complement the motif, colour, and design of the room. Fabrics made of 100 percent polyester offer excellent resistance to fading, staining, shrinking, and wrinkling.

Polycottons, a blend of polyester cotton, are less expensive than fabrics made of 100 percent polyester, but their life span is shorter, they have fewer fire-retardant qualities, and they fade more easily. While the normal recycling life span of a good bedspread should be at least 5 years, polycotton bedspreads only last from 2 to 3 years. Other factors to consider when specifying bedspreads are their fill and seaming. Fill is one of the key elements that determines the appearance of bedspreads. The number of ounces of fill per square yard should be 7 or more. Non-compressed fills are better than mechanically packed fills because of their ability to spring back to its original 'loft is greater.

Wide, seamless bedspreads are preferred to those constructed with seams because they don't come apart as easily. Bedspreads can be large enough to reach to the floor or just to cover the mattress. In this case a pleated cloth skirting called a dust ruffle may be placed between the mattress and the box spring to extend around the sides and foot of the bed. Washable bedspreads should be purchased with the guarantee that they will not shrink, fade, or wrinkle. Par levels for bedspreads should be one plus 10 percent to allow for washing and replacement.

The purpose of blankets is to act as insulators. A heavy blanket does not necessarily keep the warmth of the body from escaping through it. On the other hand, a material (even if it is light) that is tightly woven will retain body heat. However, all blankets should be porous enough to allow any moisture buildup under them to escape to the surrounding air. Wool is a delicate natural fiber that is very warm but that requires extreme care when laundered.

Cotton, on the other hand, washes easily but it is a poor insulator and shrinks up to 15 percent if not purchased preshrunk. Synthetic fibers such as acrylics and polyester, if properly constructed, are suitable to commercial operations. Acrylic fibers are warmer than polyester but not as strong. Because guests may fall asleep while smoking in bed, blankets should be fire retardant. The size of the blanket should be large enough to cover the length and width of the mattress and have some additional inches for tucking.

All mattresses should be fitted with moisture-proof covers at all times to prevent staining. Vinyl plastic covers are impermeable and can be washed like any other fabric. Their use is recommended for cribs or small cots for young children and hospital beds. Felt pads made of moisture-proof, flame-retardant, 100 per cent polyester resist shrinkage and are quite durable.

Most commercial pillows axe filled with synthetic fiber, mainly polyester. Synthetic pillows are quite common in commercial properties because they are inexpensive, easy to launder, and nonallergenic. When purchasing pillows, it is important to make sure that the fill is of good quality so that it springs back into shape easily; lumpy, heavier fills are an indication of inferior grade. The synthetic covering of the pillow must be fire retardant and stain proof and able to withstand frequent washings. Pillows with natural fills such as down and feathers are very expensive, particularly goose down.

Lodging properties should stock a few natural-fill pillows to meet the occasional request for them. Because of the price, down and feather pillows should be provided to guests on a loan basis, that is, a record should be kept in the housekeeping department of the room number where the pillows were delivered and then should be recovered after the guest's checkout. The first consideration for selecting wall coverings is that they match the general decor of the room; the second, and just as important, consideration is their durability and ease of maintenance. The two most common forms of wall coverings are paint and vinyl. The paint used to finish walls should be easy to wash with soapy water and of very good quality so that the surface doesn't require repainting after a short period of time.

Vinyl wall coverings are available in several thicknesses to suit the area to be covered; for instance, walls covered with thin layers are vulnerable to bumps from baggage and carts and should be used only to cover no-traffic areas. Heavier vinyl can withstand heavy impacts and can be used over surfaces susceptible to abrasion. Although far more expensive than paint, vinyl wall coverings generally pay for themselves because they require very little maintenance. Vinyl coverings are made by laminating the material to cotton or polycotton backings and are glued to walls using an adhesive paste. To prevent mildew from loosening the vinyl from the adhesive, the glue should contain a mildewcide. Fabric wall coverings can provide rooms and hallways with a luxurious, elegant look but they should be avoided in commercial operations because of the difficulty of cleaning or replacing them when soiled. Wallpaper should be used only if it is stain and water-resistant and allows for damp cleaning with soap and sponge.

Windows in offices, lobbies, and employee areas are usually fitted with vinyl blinds. Because of their susceptibility to fading, fabrics used for curtains must be resistant to direct sunlight. As curtains attract dust and odours, they require frequent washings and dry cleaning; for this reason, it is advisable to purchase good-quality, vinyl-coated fabrics that can retain their shape and colour for long periods of time. Curtains should be flame retardant to comply with local fire departments specifications. Drapery can be simple or quite ornate. Valances, and shirred or pinch-pleated fabrics, can add elegance and warmth to rooms, although they will require more cleaning time to keep them dust free.

In all cases, the curtain rods and cords must be sturdy to avoid damage; having batons instead of cords may reduce the chance of breakage. The housekeeping department needs major pieces of equipment to clean guest, public, and employee areas and to transport clean and soiled linen, trash, and supplies. In all cases, the department equipment used in housekeeping should be of heavy-duty quality, able to withstand rough and continuous use. Often, purveyors of chemical supplies also carry a complete line of equipment. In some cases, manufacturers have their own representatives who will describe the machines and demonstrate their performance.

Perhaps the most significant piece of housekeeping equipment is the housekeeping cart. Usually, one cart is assigned to the cleaner of each section of guestrooms and one to each janitor. The cart should be large enough and have enough shelves to carry a full complement of supplies needed in each working shift in order to avoid unnecessary trips to the linen room for additional supplies. Although sturdy, the cart must be light and maneuverable enough to be pushed by one person from door to door and from floor to floor, including pushing it into and out of service elevators. The cart should be contoured with rubber bumpers to protect walls and wall corners and have casters with brakes of superior quality.

Some carts can be purchased with side panels that can be locked in order to prevent linen and guest amenities from being exposed to whomever walks past them, thus eliminating theft. If fitted with laundry and trash bags, these should be made of heavy-duty material to withstand hard use. Plastic baskets or caddies containing guest amenities and cleaning supplies are generally placed on the top shelf of carts. Several types of vacuum cleaners are used by housekeeping. One requirement common to all of them is that they be heavy-duty and powerful enough to provide efficient, one-pass cleaning.

The typical vacuum cleaner used in guestroom carpet cleaning is upright, with one or two motors. The dual-motor type has one motor to drive the beater brush and another to provide the suction. Some useful characteristics of commercial vacuums are as follows: having collector cups or zipper receptacles instead of paper bags (some models can be messy and difficult to empty, in which case it is better to use disposable bags), long electric cable, wraparound bumpers, secondary filters to protect the vacuum motor, adjustable brush settings, three-position handles, and self-lubricating brushes.

Some vacuums are incorporated into the housekeeping cart. This arrangement, however, may cause some difficulties. Because the hoses must be long enough to reach all corners of the room, suction power may be reduced. And since the vacuum must be operated in hallways, the noise permeates throughout the area. Also, because the machine is attached to the cart, repairs and maintenance are more difficult to perform on site than in the engineering shop. Large-area vacuums are used in hallways and lobbies that contain extensive areas of carpeting.

Floor machines are designed to mechanically polish, buff, strip, scrub, grind, sand, burnish, and shampoo surfaces. Usually one multipurpose machine can be used for several tasks by changing the pad as needed to accomplish the task at hand. Burnishers are used when the property has large areas of terrazzo or tile floor. These machines are capable of burnishing up to 30,000 square feet per hour. Polishers are heavily weighted machines used to grind, sand, and polish marble and other stone floors. Scrubbers are used to automatically scrub hard or resilient surfaces by applying a stripping solution and recovering the liquid as the machine is pushed along the surface. Large scrubbers feature 40-gallon stripping solution and recovery tanks, a 34-inch self-propelled scrubber, 37-inch squeegee assembly, and can service 44,000 square feet per hour.

When large lodging properties use drinking glasses made of glass (rather than plastic), glass washers are necessary. The practice of washing housekeeping glasses in the kitchen's dishwashers is not an effective one as it is usually seen as an "encroachment" by the food and beverage department personnel. When operating a glass washer, the right type of detergent and the correct water temperature as determined by the local health department must be provided. Rather than transporting trash, soiled linen, and supplies in plastic bags, lodging properties should use light trucks or hoppers.

The three major purposes of chemicals used in the housekeeping department are to remove dirt, to destroy harmful microorganisms, and to preserve and beautify furniture, fixtures, and surfaces. Chemical cleaners are manufactured to remove soils from surfaces through chemical action. The stronger the chemical is, the better effect it will have on getting the job done. The strength of cleaning chemicals is measured on the pH scale. pH is the symbol for the logarithm of the reciprocal of hydrogen ion concentration in gram atoms per liter. Cleaning chemicals that have been enhanced with alkalis or acids to strengthen their cleaning powers can be dangerous to humans and often cannot be used on certain surfaces.

A neutral cleaner can be used for all types of jobs but its cleaning power is limited. The executive housekeeper should have adequate knowledge of the department's needs to select cleaning chemicals appropriate for each type of cleaning job to be performed regularly in the housekeeping department. Generally speaking, high-alkaline cleaners are effective degreasers while acidic cleaners are good for fighting lime and rust, which are always found in urinals and toilets. Another name for cleaners is detergents.

Detergents act chemically to emulsify dirt, holding it in suspension so it can be removed away from the surface. Synthetic detergents are easy to rinse off and often have excellent cleaning, deodorizing, and germicidal characteristics. Most cleaning detergents are made from mineral oils. All-purpose cleaners have neutral pH-balanced formulas for general-purpose cleaning jobs. They usually are synthetic detergents, often vegetable oil based, of which pine oil is very popular because of its pleasant scent and strong deodorizing power. All-purpose cleaners may have corrosion inhibitors to protect metal surfaces.

Single-purpose cleaners are heavy-duty cleaners used for specific cleaning jobs. Abrasive cleaners are cleaning powders or pastes combined with silica for tough cleaning jobs. These cleaners will scratch soft surfaces like fiberglass or porcelain. Gentler cleansers made with nonscratching calcite instead of silica greatly reduce their abrasive action.

Degreasers are highly effective cleaners, often biodegradable, that remove grease, tar, ink, food deposits, smoke film, fats and other grimy soils. Degreasers can be highly effective on concrete floors. It is important to remember that some products advertised as degreasers may be toxic and therefore not suitable for use on kitchen surfaces.

Although most all-purpose cleaners can be used as deodorizers, stronger chemicals are needed to counteract stale odours. Deodorizers can be purchased as mists, wall and urinal blocks, cup and wick, and aerosols. Glass cleaners are ammonia- and alcohol-based products that clean and provide a protective coating to glass surfaces. Glass treated with good-quality glass cleaners resist fogging caused by moisture and temperature changes and in some manner repel dust, dirt, fingerprints, and smudges. Most glass cleaners can also be used as multipurpose cleaners on chrome, stainless steel, enamel, formica, ceramic tile, and other washable surfaces.

Another purpose of housekeeping supplies is to beautify surfaces and fixtures. Furniture polishes are liquid waxes or oils or silicone-based sprays designed to protect and give shine to wood, leather, vinyl, metal, and plastic surfaces. When pigments are added to liquid furniture polish, the product helps cover nicks and scratches in wood furniture, panelling, and floors.

Most metal surfaces can be dusted, cleaned, and polished with metal polishes. Strong liquid metal polishes can remove rust, corrosion, tarnish, and grime from brass, stainless steel, copper, chrome, and aluminium. Cream polishes are quite effective in cleaning sterling silver, silver-plated utensils, nickel, and pewter.Strong acidic cleaners are needed to clean away lime and rust deposits in restroom and bathroom fixtures.

3

Cleaning

Cleaning is the complete removal of food soil using appropriate detergent chemicals under recommended conditions. It is important that personnel involved have a working understanding of the nature of the different types of food soil and the chemistry of its removal. Water comprises approximately 95-99% of cleaning and sanitising solutions. The impurities in water can drastically alter the effectiveness of a detergent or a sanitiser.

Water hardness is the most important chemical property with a direct effect on cleaning and sanitising efficiency. Water pH ranges generally from pH 5 to 8.5. This range is of no serious consequence to most detergents and sanitisers. However, highly alkaline or highly acidic water may require additional buffering agents. Water can also contain significant numbers of microorganisms.

Food soil is generally defined as unwanted matter on food-contact surfaces. Soil is visible or invisible. The primary source of soil is from the food product being handled. However, minerals from water residue and residues from cleaning compounds contribute to films left on surfaces. Microbiological biofilms also contribute to the soil buildup on surfaces. Since soils vary widely in composition, no one detergent is capable of removing all types. Many complex films contain: combinations of food components, surface oil or dust, insoluble cleaner components, and insoluble hard-water salts. These films vary in their solubility properties depending upon such factors as heat effect, age, dryness, time, etc. It is essential that personnel involved have an understanding of the nature of the soil to be removed before selecting a detergent or cleaning regime. Therule of thumb is that acid cleaners dissolve alkaline soils (minerals) and alkaline cleaners dissolve acid soils and food wastes.

Improper use of detergents can actually "set" soils, making them more difficult to remove (e.g., acid cleaners can precipitate protein). Many films and biofilms require more sophisticated cleaners which are amended with oxidising agents (such as chlorinated detergents) for removal. The physical condition of the soil deposits also effects its solubility. Freshly precipitated soil in a cool or cold solution is usually more easily dissolved than an old, dried, or baked-on deposit, or a complex film.

Fat: Fat usually is present as an emulsion and can generally be rinsed away with hot water above the melting point. More difficult fat and oil residues can be removed with alkaline detergents which have good emulsifying or saponifying ingredients.

Protein: In the food industry, proteins are by far the most difficult soils to remove. In fact, casein (a major milk protein) is used for its adhesive properties in many glues and paints. Food proteins range from more simple proteins, which are easy to remove, to more complex proteins, which are very difficult to remove. Heat-denatured proteins can be extremely difficult.

Carbohydrate: Simple sugars are readily soluble in warm water and are quite easily removed. Starch residues, individually, are also easily removed with mild detergents. Starches associated with proteins or fatscan usually be easily removed by highly alkaline detergents.

Mineral Salt: Mineral salts can be either relatively easy to remove, or be highly troublesome deposits or films. Calcium and magnesium are involved in some of the most difficult mineral films. Under conditions involving heat and alkaline pH, calcium and magnesium can combine with bicarbonates to form highly insoluble complexes. Other difficult deposits contain iron or manganese. Salt films can also cause corrosion of some surfaces. Difficult salt films require an acid cleaner (especially organic acids which form complexes with these salts) for removal.

Microbiological films: Under certain conditions, microorgranisms (bacteria, yeasts, and molds) can form invisible films (biofilms) on surfaces. Biofilms can be difficult to remove and usually require cleaners as well as sanitisers with strong oxidising properties.

Lubricating greases and oils: These deposits (insoluble in water, alkali, or acid) can often be melted with hot water or steam, but oftenleave a residue. Surfactants can be used to emulsify the residue to make it suspendable in water and flushable.

Cleanability Surface

The cleanability of the surface is a primary consideration in evaluating cleaning effectiveness. Stainless steel is the preferred surface for food equipment and is specified in many industry and regulatory design and construction standards. Other "soft" metals (aluminum, brass, copper, or mild steel), or nonmetallic surfaces (plastics, or rubber) are also used on food contact surfaces. Surfaces of soft metals and nonmetallic materials are generally less corrosion- resistant and care should be exercised in their cleaning.

Aluminum is readily attacked by acids as well as highly alkaline cleaners which can render the surface non-cleanable. Plastics are subject to stress cracking and clouding from prolonged exposure to corrosive food materials or cleaning agents. Hard wood (maple or equivalent) or sealed wood surfaces should only be used in limited applications such as cutting boards or cutting tables provided the surface is maintained in good repair. Such surfaces are more difficult to clean or sanitise, and may no longer be cleanable.

Detergents

Detergents and cleaning compounds are usually composed of mixtures of ingredients that interact with soils in several ways. In some detergents, specific enzymes are added to catalytically react with, and degrade, specific food soil components. The primary physically active ingredients are the surface active compounds termed surfactants. These organic molecules have general structural characteristicwhere a portion of the structure is hydrophilic (water- loving) and a portion is hydrophobic (not reactive with water). Such molecules function in detergents by promoting the physical cleaning actions through: emulsification, penetration, spreading, foaming, and wetting. It is a common practice to blend surfactant ingredients to optimize their properties. However, because of precipitation problems, cationic and anionic surfactants cannot be blended.

The most common inorganic acids used include: phosphoric, nitric, sulfamic, sodium acid sulfate, and hydrochloric. Organic acids, such as hydroxyacetic, citric, and gluconic, are also in use. Acid detergents are often used in a two-step sequential cleaning regime with alkaline detergents. Acid detergents are also used for the prevention or removal of stone films (mineral stone, beer stone, or milk stone).

Water conditioners are used to prevent the build-up of various mineral deposits (water hardness, etc.). These chemicals are usually sequestering agents or chelating agents. Sequestering agents form soluble complexes with calcium and magnesium. Examples are sodium tripolyphosphate, tetra-potassium pyrophosphate, organo-phosphates, and polyelectrolytes. Chelating agents include sodium gluconate and ethylene diamine tetracetic acid (EDTA).

Enzyme-based detergents, which are amended with enzymes such as amylases and other carbohydrate-degrading enzymes, proteases, and lipases, are finding acceptance in specialised food industry applications. The primary advantages of enzyme detergents are that they are more environmentally friendly and often require less energy input (less hot water in cleaning). Uses of most enzyme cleaners are usually limited to unheated surfaces (e.g., cold-milk surfaces). However, new generation enzyme cleaners (currently under evaluation) are expected to have broader application.

Fillers add bulk or mass, or dilute dangerous detergent formulations which are difficult to handle. Strong alkalis are often diluted with fillers for ease and safety of handling. Water is used in liquid formulations as a filler. Sodium chloride or sodium sulfate are often fillers in powdered detergent formuations.

Effective Sanitising

Effectiveness sanitising is dependant upon a number of factors including: initial contamination load, humidity, pH, temperature, and time. The use of steam as a sanitising process has limited application. It is generally expensive compared to alternatives, and it is difficult to regulate and monitor contact temperature and time. Further, the byproducts of steam condensation can complicate cleaning operations. Hot-water sanitising—through immersion (small parts, knives, etc.), spray (dishwashers), or circulating systems—is commonly used. The time required is determined by the temperature of the water.

The primary advantages of hot-water sanitisation are: relatively inexpensive, easy to apply and readily available, generally effective over a broad range of microorganisms, relatively non-corrosive, and penetratesinto cracks and crevices. Hot-water sanitisation is a slow process which requires come-up and cool-down time; can have high energy costs; and has certain safety concerns for employees. The process also has the disadvantages of forming or contributing to film formations, and shortening the life of certain equipment or parts thereof (gaskets, etc.).

The registration of chemical sanitisers and antimicrobial agents for use on food and food product contact surfaces, and on nonproduct contact surfaces, is through the U.S. Environmental Protection Agency (EPA). Thus, any antimicrobial agent and its maximum usage level for direct use on food or on food product contact surfaces must be approved by the FDA.

Prior to the sanitisation process, all surfaces must be clean and thoroughly rinsed to remove any detergent residue. An unclean surface cannot be sanitised. Since the effectiveness of sanitisation requires direct contact with the microorganisms, the surface should be free of cracks, pits, or crevices which can harbor microorganisms. Surfaces which contain biofilms cannot be effectively sanitised.

Generally, the activity of a sanitiser increases with increased concentration. However, a leveling off occurs at high concentrations. A common misconception regarding chemicals is that "if a little is good, more is better". Using sanitiser concentrations above recommendations does not sanitiser better and, in fact, can be corrosive to equipment and in the long run lead to less cleanability.

Sanitisers are dramatically affected by the pH of the solution. Many chlorine sanitisers, for example, are almost ineffective at pH values above 7.5. Organic and/or inorganic inactivators may react chemically with sanitisers giving rise to non-germicidal products. Some of these inactivators are present in detergent residue. Thus, it is important that surfaces be rinsed prior to sanitisation. The microbiological load can affect sanitiser activity. Also, the type of microorganism present is important. Spores are more resistant than vegetative cells. Certain sanitisers are more active against gram positive than gram negative microorganisms, and vice versa.

Chlorine, in its various forms, is the most commonly used sanitiser in food processing and handling applications. Commonly used chlorine compounds include: liquid chlorine, hypochlorites, inorganic chloramines, and organic chloramines. Chlorine-based sanitisers form hypochlorous acid (HOCl, the most active form) in solution. Available chlorine (the amount of HOCl present) is a function of pH. At pH 5, nearly all is in the form of HOCl. At pH 7.0, approximately 75% is HOCl. The maximumallowable level for no-rinse applications is 200ppm available chlorine, but recommended usage levels vary.

For hypochlorites, an exposure time of 1 min at a minimum concentration of 50ppm and a temperature of 24°C (75°F) is recommended. For each 10°C (18°F) drop in temperature, a doubling of exposure time is recommended. For chloramines, 200ppm for 1 min is recommended. Chlorine compounds are broad spectrum germicides which act on microbial membranes, inhibit cellular enzymes involved in glucose metabolism, have a lethal effect on DNA, and oxidise cellular protein.

Chlorine has activity at low temperature, is relatively cheap, and leaves minimal residue or film on surfaces. The activity of chlorine is dramatically affected by such factors as pH, temperature, and organic load. However, chlorine is less affected by water hardness when compared to other sanitisers. The major disadvantage to chlorine compound is corrosiveness to many metal surfaces. Health and safety concerns can occur due to skin irritation and mucous membrane damage in confined areas.

At low pH (below 4.0), deadly Cl_2 (mustard gas) can form. In recent years, concerns have also been raised about the use of chlorine as a drinking water disinfectant and as an antimicrobial with direct food contact (meat, poultry and shellfish). This concern is based upon the involvement of chlorine in the formation of potentially carcinogenic trihalomethanes (THMs) under appropriate conditions. While chlorine's benefits as a sanitiser far outweigh these risks, it is under scrutiny.

Chlorine dioxide (ClO_2) is currently being considered as a replacement for chlorine, since it appears to be more environmentally friendly. Stabilised ClO_2 has FDA approval for most applications in sanitising equipment or for use as a foam for environmental and non-food contact surfaces. Approval has also been granted for use in flume waters in fruits and vegetable operations and in poultry process waters. ClO_2 has 2.5 times the oxidising power of chlorine and, thus, less chemical is required.

Typical use concentrations range from 1to 10ppm. ClO_2's primary disadvantages are worker safety and toxicity. Its highly concentrated gases can be explosive and exposure risks to workers is higher thanthat for chlorine. Its rapid decomposition in the presence of light, or at temperatures greater than 50°C (122°F) makes on-site generation a recommended practice. Use of iodine as an antimicrobial agents dates back to the 1800s.

This sanitiser exists in many forms and usually exists with a surfactant as a carrier. These mixtures are termed iodophors. The most active agent is the dissociated free iodine. This form is most prevalent at low pH. The amount of dissociation from the surfactant is dependent upon the type of surfactant. Iodine solubility is very limited in water.

Generally recommended usage for iodophors is 12.5 to 25ppm for 1 min. It is generally thought that the bactericidal activity of iodine is through direct halogenation of proteins. More recent theories have centered upon cell wall damage and destruction of microbial enzyme activity. Iodophors, like chlorine compounds, have a very broad spectrum: being active against bacteria, viruses, yeasts, molds, fungi, and protozoans.

Iodine is highly temperature-dependent and vaporizes at 120°F. Thus, it is limited to lower temperature applications. The degree to which iodophors are affected by environmental factors is highly dependant upon properties of the surfactant used in the formulation. Iodophors are generally less affected by organic matter and water hardness than chlorine. However, loss of activity is pronounced at high pH. Iodine has a long history of use in wound treatment.

Since Quaternary Ammonium Compounds (QACs) are positively charged cations, their mode of action is related to their attraction to negatively charged materials such as bacterial proteins. It is generally accepted that the mode of action is at the membrane function. The carbon length of R-group side chain is, generally, directly related with sanitiser activity in QACs. However, because of the lower solubility in QACs composed of large carbon chains, these sanitisers may have lower activity than short chain structures. QACs are active and stable over a broad temperature range. Because they are surfactants, they possess some detergency. Thus, they are less affected by light soil than are other sanitisers.

However, heavy soil dramatically decreases activity. QACs generally have higher activity at alkaline pH. While lack of tolerance to hard water is often listed as a major disadvantage of QACs when compared to chlorine, some QACs are fairly tolerant of hard water. Activity can be improved by the use of EDTA as a chelator. QACs are effective against bacteria, yeasts, mold, and viruses. An advantage of QACs in some applications is that they leave a residual antimicrobial film. However, this would be a disadvantage in operations such as cultured dairy products, cheese, beer, etc. where microbial starter cultures are used.

QACs are generally more active against gram positive than gram negative bacteria. They are not highly effective against bacteriophages. Their incompatibility with certain detergents makes thorough rinsing following cleaning operations imperative.Further, many QAC formulations can cause foaming problems in CIP applications. Under recommended usage and precautions, QACs pose little toxicity or safety risks. Thus, they are in common use as environmental fogs and as room deodorisers.

However, care should be exercised in handling concentrated solutions or use as environmental fogging agents. Like QACs, acid-anionic sanitisers are surface-active sanitisers. These formulations include an inorganic acid plus a surfactant, and are often used for the dual function of acid rinse and sanitisation. Whereas QACs are positively charged, these sanitisers are negatively charged. Their activity is moderately affected by water hardness. Their low use pH, detergency, stability, low odor potential, and non-corrosiveness makes them highly desirable in some applications.

Fatty acid or carboxylic acid sanitisers were developed in the 1980s. Typical formulations include fatty acids plus other acids (phosphoric acids, organic acids). These agents also have the dual function of acid rinse and sanitisation. The major advantage over acid anionics is lower foaming potential. These sanitisers have a broad range of activity, are highly stable in dilute form, are stable to organic matter, and are stable to high temperature applications. These sanitisers have low activity above pH 3.5 - 4.0, are not very effective against yeasts and molds, and some formulations lose activity at temperatures below 10°C (50°F).

Peroxides or peroxy compounds contain at least one pair of covalently bonded oxygen atoms (-O-O-)and are divided into two groups: the inorganic group, containing hydrogen peroxide (HP) and related compounds; and the organic group, containing peroxyacetic acid (PAA) and related compounds. The primary mode of action for HP is through creating an oxidising environment and generation of singlet or superoxide oxygen (SO).

HP is fairly broad spectrum with slightly higher activity against gram-negative than gram-positive organisms. High concentrations of HP (5% and above) can be an eye and skin irritant. Thus, high concentrations should be handled with care. Peroxyacetic Acid (PAA) has been known for its germicidal properties for a long time. However, it has only found food-industry application in recent years and is being promoted as a potential chlorine replacement.

PAA is relatively stable at use strengths of 100 to 200ppm. Other desirable properties include: absence of foam and phosphates, low corrosiveness, tolerance to hard water, and favorable biodegradability. PAA solutions have been shown to be useful in removing biofilms. While precise mode of action mechanisms have not been determined, it is generally theorised that the PAA reaction with microorganisms is similar to that of HP. PAA, however, is highly active against both gram- positive and gram-negative microorganisms. The germicidal activity of PAA is dramatically affected by pH. Any pH increase above 7-8 drastically reduces the activity. PAA has a pungent odor and the concentrated product (40%) is a highly toxic, potent irritant, and powerful oxidiser. Thus, care must be used in its use.

Restroom Cleaning

Today's marketplace of custodial equipment affords housekeeping managers many advantages in cleaning restrooms, compared with the days of the traditional mop, bucket and wringer. The traditional method, though still in use, is increasingly falling behind the new technologies. Some new systems are simple, while others are more complex, but most systems enhance the performance of cleaning chemicals - if, in fact, any chemicals are used at all - and all while enabling managers to minimise complaints by effectively cleaning restrooms.

Vapour Cleaning systems are becoming increasingly popular. The systems use no chemicals. Instead, they use a tank that superheats the water, and operators spray the resulting steam onto the dirty areas with a special wand that features an applicator to which cleaning towels might be attached. The operator wipes all surfaces with the superheated vapor, changing the cloth as it becomes soiled. The units also have special heads that allow for crevice cleaning.

In addition to using these units for cleaning restrooms, cleaning crews also can use them for cleaning kitchens because the steam easily breaks down the grease. Also, when using the wand and towel attachment, the units might be effective in cleaning dirt off walls. Manufacturers of some of these systems claim that the units require no chemicals, but housekeeping managers should familiarise themselves with the claims and the infection-control needs of their facility.

Also, operators need to be aware that the vapor is hot and that handles of some wands might become hot. As a result, they will need to wear appropriate personal protective equipment. Several manufacturers now market restroom cleaning kits that might include a cleaning cart, a bucket and a series of extension handles with associated specialised mop heads and attachments. The cart has space for storing cleaning supplies and paper products. Increasingly, crews are replacing old cotton-string mops with microfiber flat mops that are easier to use, lighter and enable aggressive cleaning of the surface. The restroom cleaning kits give the person cleaning restrooms all of the necessary products they might need on the job site.

Some advocates of microfiber cleaning cloths say that the cloths eliminate or mitigate the need for cleaning chemicals. Realistically, crews often can enhance their cleaning efforts in restrooms by applying the appropriate chemicals during the cleaning process. Specialised power washers for cleaning restrooms have been available for several years now.

Generally, the power washer is cart-mounted for carrying limited cleaning supplies and might come in various sizes. Basically, after the floor has been swept, the unit allows the operator to power-wash the restroom from ceiling to floor and to air dry the room before use. These units have specialised chemicals, applied through a solution pick-up hose, that afford deep cleaning and drying of surfaces without leaving spots, much like an effective dishwashing agent.

More advanced units not only can allow an operator to power spray a room but can also pick up the residue solution after cleaning to minimise the time that a restroom is out of service. When using these units, operators need use all appropriate safety precautions. For example, crews should not spray chemicals into electrical outlets, and they should make sure that paper goods are adequately protected from solution overspray.

When used correctly, these units really do deliver deep cleaning to restrooms. Manufacturers have provided a new generation of equipment for housekeeping managers to specify to improve the level of restroom cleaning in their facilities. Several can help minimise the use of chemicals. Housekeeping managers who want to curtail complaints concerning their facilities' restrooms and minimise the impact of cleaning chemicals and processes on the environment have more options than ever today. They can achieve these goals by learning about those options. Today's environmentally friendly chemicals and equipment are increasingly cost competitive, have increased efficacy, limit damage to the environment and minimise costs to an organisation for disposal of chemicals.

The proper maintenance of a health care facility increases the awareness of other employees of the necessity of good sanitary practices. Good housekeeping practices increase moral and public relations. No one wants to work in an area that smells or is dirty. Sanitation depends upon cleaning thoroughness. There should be procedures in writing to fit each area of the facility such as walls, floors, windows, beds, furniture, draperies, carpets, waste containers, bathrooms, equipment, stairs, elevators, special-care equipment and handling of infectious waste for disposal.

Role of Cleaning Workers

Maids and housekeeping cleaners perform any combination of light cleaning duties to maintain private households or commercial establishments, such as hotels, restaurants, and hospitals, clean and orderly. In hotels, aside from cleaning and maintaining the premises, maids and housekeeping cleaners may deliver ironing boards, cribs, and rollaway beds to guests' rooms. In hospitals, they also may wash bedframes, brush mattresses, make beds, and disinfect and sterilise equipment and supplies with germicides and sterilising equipment.

Janitors, maids, and cleaners use various equipment, tools, and cleaning materials. For one job they may need a mop and bucket, for another an electric polishing machine and a special cleaning solution. Improved building materials, chemical cleaners, and power equipment have made many tasks easier and less time consuming, but cleaning workers must learn the proper use of equipment and cleaners to avoid harming floors, fixtures, and themselves. Cleaning supervisors coordinate, schedule, and supervise the activities of janitors and cleaners.

They assign tasks and inspect building areas to see that work has been done properly, issue supplies and equipment, and inventory stocks to ensure that an adequate amount of supplies is present. They also screen and hire job applicants, train new and experienced employees, and recommend promotions, transfers, or dismissals.

Supervisors may prepare reports concerning the occupancy of rooms, hours worked, and department expenses. Some also perform cleaning duties. Cleaners and servants in private households dust and polish furniture; sweep, mop, and wax floors; vacuum; and clean ovens, refrigerators, and bathrooms. They also may wash dishes, polish silver, and change and make beds. Some wash, fold, and iron clothes; a few wash windows.

Supervisors conduct inspections to ensure that the building is cleaned properly and the team is functioning efficiently. Building cleaning workers usually work inside heated, well-lighted buildings. However, they sometimes work outdoors, sweeping walkways, mowing lawns, or shoveling snow. Working with machines can be noisy, and some tasks, such as cleaning bathrooms and trash rooms, can be dirty and unpleasant. Janitors may suffer cuts, bruises, and burns from machines, handtools, and chemicals. They spend most of their time on their feet, sometimes lifting or pushing heavy furniture or equipment.

Janitors and cleaners work in nearly every type of establishment and held about 2.3 million jobs. They accounted for about 57 percent of all building cleaning workers. About 28 percent worked for firms supplying building maintenance services on a contract basis, 21 percent were employed in educational institutions, and 2 percent worked in hotels. Other employers included hospitals, restaurants, religious institutions, manufacturing firms, government agencies, and operators of apartment buildings, office buildings, and other types of real estate.

Maids and housekeepers held about 1.5 million jobs. Hotels, motels, and other traveler accommodations employed the most maids and housekeepers-27 percent-while private households employed the second most: 25 percent. Eight percent were employed in hospitals; and, a similar percentage worked in nursing and other residential care facilities.

Most building cleaners learn their skills on the job. Usually, beginners work with an experienced cleaner, doing routine cleaning. As they gain more experience, they are assigned more complicated tasks. In some cities, programs run by unions, government agencies, or employers teach janitorial skills. Students learn how to clean buildings thoroughly and efficiently, how to select and safely use various cleansing agents, and how to operate and maintain machines, such as wet and dry vacuums, buffers, and polishers.

Dish Washing

Maybe you've never seen what happens to a sinkful of

dishes left to sit, but it isn't pretty. Smells, stains, and odd fungal growth usually go with forgotten dirty dishes. Cleaning dishes daily is the best choice all around.

Tools for Dish Washing

Dishpans: If you don't have a double sink, a dishpan can be used to rinse or hold your dishes during the washing process. Choose one that is a good size, but remember if it's too big, it will make filling and emptying the pan a messy difficult process.

Dishrack: Dishracks prevent water from collecting and pooling in your newly clean dishes. They prevent bacteria growth and help protect dishes from banging into one another. Many models now have fold down prongs for easier storage when the dishes are done. Choose a dishrack with a sloping bottom mat to allow water to easily drain off into a sink.

Dish Towels: Dish towels will be necessary to buff out spots and dry still wet dishes. Remember to make the rinsing water as hot as possible to allow the dishes to quickly airdry. Airdrying is more sanitary than cloth drying. Dish towels pick up bacteria that is then transferred to every dish dried. Always use clean dishcloths to dry dishes. Lint-free cloths may be needed for silverware.

Mats: A rubber mat placed in the bottom of the sink helps prevent breakage when dishes are loaded and moved around.

Scrapers, scrubbers, and sponges: Steel wool pads, plastic scrubbers, and double sided sponges may all be useful during dishwashing. Throw away steel wool pads and scrubbers when they show excessive signs of wear. Allow sponges to air dry after use.

Rubber Gloves: Rubber gloves increase handling power and protect hands. Find a good pair of rubber gloves, disposable gloves, or latex free gloves and protect your hands.

Dishcloths: As with sponges, dishcloths must not be allowed to sit for long periods of time in dishwater. Remember to launder your dishcloths frequently to prevent bacteria, staining, and odors.

Dishliquids: Dish liquids come in many scents, specialties, and varieties. Be sure not to add too much, which only makes washing and rinsing dishes more difficult. Check out some environmentally friendly options.

Dish washing is made a lot easier by following the right order with the right tools. Find out what you need for easy foolproof dish washing. Try this easy how-to to help with your dish washing needs.

1. Prepare the dishes

To avoid polluting your sink of water, begin by scraping the dishes of excess food. Stack the dishes in preparation for washing. Tough stuck on foods may need to be soaked first before washing.

2. Prepare the water

Make sure you use the correct water temperature. Add dish soap and the water will be ready to begin dish washing.

3. Wash the lightest soiled items first.

This usually includes glasses, cups, and flatware. Washing these items first keeps your water fresher and ready to tackle bigger jobs.

4. Wash plates, bowls, and serving dishes.

Remember to scrape these items before washing. Wash gently. Keep an eye out for when you should change the dish washing water.

5. Wash cooking dishes.

Any tough food should have been soaking already, making this dish washing go more smoothly. Wash the pans thoroughly, and you're done washing. Don't forget to clean the bottoms of pans. Any oily residue left will burn onto the bottom of the pan at the next cooking session.

6. Rinse the dish washing suds and residue from the dishes.

If you have a double sink, dish washing is a snap. Use the second sink to rinse of the dish washing suds from the dishes. If you don't have a double sink, you can use a dish pan filled with hot water to rinse/dip your dishes clean.

7. Dry dishes.

If you've used the right water temperature, the dishes will dry quickly on their own. In some instances, you may have to use a dish towel. Make sure the towel is clean. Change the towel when it becomes damp.

8. Put away dishes

Put all of the dishes away. Leaving them sitting out will expose your dishes to bacteria and germs that were just scrubbed off of them.

9. Wipe down the sink and your tools

Wipe down the sink, dish drainer, and dishpan. Any rags,

dish cloths, or sponges need to be left out to air dry, or thrown into the washing machine. Remember to replace sponges and rags frequently. Put away your supplies and you're done.

Tips:

1. Dishes wash easily if you keep them under the water while scrubbing them. Particles lift away. Bring the dish out of the water to check for missed spots.
2. Stacking a few dishes in the sink at a time allows dishes a few minutes of soaking time while you work on washing another dish.
3. Try drying pots and pans with a paper towel to reduce residue from the pan staining the dishcloth.
4. Don't allow aluminum to soak while dishwashing. Doing so can darken the finish.
5. Dish washing silverware can be tricky. Use a lint free cloth for drying silverware.

Laundry Washing

Not every family needs to wash laundry daily, but many of us find that at least a daily load of laundry is necessary. A daily load can help prevent a mad dash to find a baseball jersey in the bottom of a hamper.

Stain Removal

Removing stains can sometimes seem like a complex algebra problem. By the time you determine the stain type, origin of the stain, fabric type and color schemed you can feel pessimistic about stain removal. Try these 10 simple stain removal rules to get your laundry in shape.

1. Act quickly.

Fresh stains make stain removal an easy task. Give yourself the upper hand by treating stains as promptly after they happen as possible. If your stains are on a non-washable fabric, take them to the dry cleaners as soon as possible. Be sure to point out the stain to the dry cleaner and describe the nature of the stain. This makes the likelihood of stain removal success greater.

2. Follow the directions.

Follow the directions on any stain removal products you use. Don't forget to follow washing directions on the stained clothes.

3. Test in a hidden area.

Don't forget to test any stain removal methods on a hidden seam or other inconspicous spot. You want to check for colorfastness before applying a treatment to a large or noticeable area of the clothing. Do not use if the color changes.

4.Remove stains from the back.

Place the stained garment with the stain upside down on top of a clean white cloth. Apply stain treatment to the back of the stain. Our goal is to remove the stain from the clothing instead of making it travel all the way through to the other side. Make sure to move the stained clothing to a fresh spot as the stain begins to remove itself from the clothing and onto the cloth.

5. Be careful with dry cleaning solvents.

Make sure to rinse thoroughly, and allow to air dry any garment that's had dry cleaning solvents used on it. These solvents can be a fire hazard in a washing machine. Remember never to put dry cleaning solvents directly into the washing machine.

6. Be wary of even color removal with bleach.

Bleaching only one stained spot on a garment may result in uneven color removal for the entire garment. Consider using the appropriate bleach listed in the garment tag to bleach the entire garment.

7. Don't mix stain removal products.

Mixing different chemicals can cause toxic odors and mixed results on your clothing.

8. Wash stain treated items.

Remember to thoroughly wash items that have treated with stain removal products to remove product residue and also the stain residue.

9. Be patient.

Stain removal can take time. Sometimes repeat treatments may be required. Be sure to thoroughly check the garment before drying to determine if a repeat treatment is necessary. Drying will cause a stain to set.

10. Some stains won't leave.

For some stains, no stain removal idea or tip can get rid of them without damaging the clothing or its color. But take heart in the fact that the other 9 general stain removal tips will give you a fighting chance against all the stains in your laundry basket. Just a few simple guidelines can take the guesswork out of stain removal.

Sorting

Sorting is the easiest part of washing clothes, right? Wrong. Sorting is the most difficult and time consuming part of laundry. If done incorrectly sorting ruins clothes and can damage machines. When done properly sorting saves invaluable time, energy, and money. There are 6 main things to look for when sorting laundry. Actually placing the clothing in the proper pile is only one of them.

1. Check clothing tags.

Read the tags thoroughly to determine how the clothes should be washed dried and ironed. Most items will have mainly normal washing instructions. You might be surprised though that you have items that are meant to be hand washed or not dried in the drier. Set these items aside in their own "Special Care" pile. Check here for Fabric Link's guide to Fabric Care Symbols.

2. Turn clothing right side out.

Make sure none of the legs of your pants, or arms of your shirts are stuck in the garment improperly. If you are washing overalls, take the time now to clasp the latches of the overalls to their proper buttons, keeping them from getting broken, stretched or ripped. If you had any clothing tags that instructed you to wash the clothing inside out, make sure you remembered to do so.

3. Check all pockets.

It's best to have a bowl nearby to hold the contents of your pockets. Failing to check pockets can leave some nasty surprises.

4. Check for sewing repairs.

Make sure there aren't any loose threads, rips, button

repairs, or other sewing repairs. If you find any, repair them before you wash the clothes. Washing them with problems will only make the problems bigger.

5. Check for stains

They will need to be pretreated or soaked before washing and drying. If you dry a stain, you'll most likely have a stain for life.

6. Sort the clothing.

There are many different methods to sorting. Some people sort by color. Others sort by fabric type. There are some adventurous souls who actually never sort clothing. Your sorting method will likely be determined by the size of your family and contents of your wardrobes. Here are some of the sorting categories that may demand special attention.

Whites- Whites go separate because we want them to stay white. One red sock that isn't colorfast can turn an entire white load pink. More often than not whites need a warmer water temperature than other clothing to ensure proper cleaning.

Reds and or Bright Colors- Colorfast pinks, purples, reds, and oranges can be mixed together to make a full load.

Some people like to sort everything else into its color category to get a nice mix of small and large items for each load. For example, with a large family you may end up with a blue load, green load, khaki load, black load, etc. If your items are colorfast, (most clothing will be) you can combine colors together.

4

Laundry Facility

Every large hotel has in-house laundry facility. Laundry contributes around 1 to 2% to the total hotel (65% of average occupancy in a year) financial turnover.It consumes around 2 to 5% of the total hotel electricity. Out of which, washing accounts approximately 35% and drying & finishing accounts for 65%. The Repair and Maintenance expenditure of laundry equipment's is around 15 to 20% of the total laundry earnings. The expenditure on chemical usage for laundry is around 15 to 30% of the total laundry earnings

Laundry operation in a hotel consumes enormous amount of resource (both hot and cold water, electricity, steam, chemicals) there by generating a large amount of wastewater (having phosphates and detergents). Chemicals used for dry cleaning are hazardous in nature and require safety precautions for handling.

To meet the high standard of service (some hotels have laundry service for out side guest also) in the hospitality world, laundry is put in operation for around 16 to 20 hours a day and during peak season the operation extends round the clock. A periodic performance monitoring and measurement is required to understand the different type of resource consumption per unit of laundry processed. The performance indicators for laundry department is

i) Electricity consumed (kWh/Ton of linen processed per day)

ii) Steam Consumed (kg/Ton of linen processed per day)

iii) Total water consumed (m3/Ton of linen processed per day)

iii) Chemicals consumed (kg/Ton of linen processed per day)

iv) Laundry R&M expenditure Vs Guest laundry earning (Ratio)

v) Laundry R&M expenditure Vs Total hotel turnover (Ratio)

History of Laundry

Laundry was probably first done by immersing cloth in streams and letting the stream carry away the materials causing stains and smells. In many Third-World countries and rural regions, laundry may still be done this way. Agitation helps remove the dirt, so the laundry is often rubbed, twisted, or slapped against flat rocks.

Various chemicals may be used increase the solvent power of water, such as the compounds in soaproot or yucca-root used by Native American tribes. Soap, a compound made from lye (from wood-ash) and fat, is an ancient and very common laundry aid. However, modern washing machines typically use powdered or liquid laundry detergent in place of soap.

When there were no streams to use for laundry, laundry was done in water-tight vats or vessels. Sometimes large metal cauldrons were filled with fresh water and heated over a fire; boiling water was even more effective than cold in removing dirt. The washboard, a corrugated slab of a hard material such as metal, replaced rocks as a surface for loosening soil.

Once clean, the clothes were wrung out—twisted to remove most of the water. Then they were hung up on poles or clotheslines to dry, or sometimes just spread out on clean grass.

The Industrial Revolution completely transformed laundry technology. First came the mangle (wringer US), in the 18th century—two long rollers in a frame and a crank to revolve them. A laundry-worker took sopping wet clothing and cranked it through the mangle, compressing the cloth and expelling the excess water. The mangle was much quicker than hand twisting.

In the early 20th century inventors further mechanised the laundry process with various washing machines. Typically, these machines used an electrically-powered agitator to replace tedious hand rubbing against a washboard. The earliest machines were simply a tub on legs, with a hand-operated mangle on top. Later the mangle too was electrically powered, then replaced by a perforated double tub, which spun out the excess water in a spin cycle. Laundry drying was also mechanised, with dryers. Dryers were also spinning perforated tubs, but they blew heated air rather than water.

Modern Laundry

Washing machines and dryers are now fixtures in homes around the world. Apartment buildings and dormitories often have laundry rooms, where residents share washing machines and dryers. Usually the machines are set to run only when coins in appropriate amounts are inserted in a coin-slot.

Use a car as agitator. If clothes are put in a water-tight container, with soap or detergent, and the container is placed in the trunk of a car or the bed of a pick-up truck, a few hours of stop-and-start driving or a stretch of bumpy road will agitate nicely. The clothes may then be rinsed and dried. This method is said to be used by some ranchers in the Western part of the United States.

Laundry Detergent

Laundry detergent is a substance which is a type of detergent that is added when one is washing laundry to help get the laundry cleaner. It is often colloquially called laundry soap or simply detergent or soap and it helps wash the fabric in a manner rather analogous to the way soap helps wash hands, other parts of the body, or other things cleaner than washing with water alone. Laundry detergent has traditionally been a powdered or granular solid, but the use of liquid laundry detergents has gradually increased over the years, and these days use of liquid detergent equals or even exceeds use of solid detergent.

Because it is consumed when it is used, the sale of laundry detergent is a rather large business. There are many different kinds or brands of laundry detergent sold, many of them claiming some special qualities as selling points. Each brand has its own instructions on how to use it and what amount to use written on the container it comes in. These days, some brands of laundry detergent purport to be more concentrated and can be added in smaller amounts.

The detergent can be added onto the laundry or to the wash water at the start of the wash, or it can be added beforehand or soon after starting the wash into a special compartment in a washing machine made for that purpose, to be flushed into the wash by the wash water. Often bleach is a separate additive to the wash, but there are laundry detergents which have bleach already blended in with them. The detergent is soluble in water and makes the water wash the laundry better along with agitation or tumbling. The detergent does its work and is needed during the initial "Wash" cycle to separate the dirt or soil out from the fabric. The purpose of the rinses which follow is to rinse the detergent residue from the laundry as well as to remove the dirt suspended in the wash water by replacing the initial wash water with fresh water.

Separate stain pre-treatment products are sometimes available to be added directly to stained areas of fabrics. However, undiluted liquid laundry detergent or a paste of solid detergent made by mixing in a little water may be used to pre-treat heavily soiled or stained areas of the fabric by scrubbing in the detergent prior to the wash. Removal of certain types of stains is tough and can be achieved only with varying degrees of success. Also, special oxidizer washing products have become available in liquid or solid granular form. Such solid products often contain sodium percarbonate and the liquid products often contain hydrogen peroxide. Some laundry detergent is specially sold for wool fabric.

Containers and Sizes

Solid laundry detergent is commonly sold in cardboard boxes. The size of the boxes can vary from small single-use boxes sold from vending machines in laundromats to large economy-size boxes. In some cases, plastic measuring scoops have been included inside the boxes. Liquid detergent is sold in plastic bottles, usually high density polyethylene or sometimes PET or other kinds. Again, various sizes are available. On large size bottles, a handle to carry the bottle is often pre-formed as part of the bottle. The bottle caps are often made large enough so they can be used as cups for measuring out the liquid detergent.

A key ingredient in both solid and liquid laundry detergents is surfactant. A surfactant is a substance which, when added to water, significantly reduces the surface tension of the water. This effect allows water to wash surfaces better. There are many different types of organic compounds which can function as surfactants. Most surfactants are thick, viscous liquids, but some are soft, waxy or greasy solids.

Surfactants typically have somewhat longer molecules which may or may not have a charge. Surfactants with uncharged molecules are non-ionic surfactants. Surfactants with positively charged molecules (or ions) are cationic surfactants. Surfactants with negatively charged molecules (or ions) are anionic surfactants. Most brands of laundry detergent have anionic or nonionic surfactants or a mixture of the two, although cationic surfactants have been used in laundry detergents. The use of cationic and anionic surfactants together is incompatible in the same detergent.

In powdered or granular solid detergents, the surfactant is soaked into the solid ingredients. In liquid laundry detergents, liquid or even solid surfactant are blended into the liquid detergent. There is usually a limit on how much liquid surfactant can soak into powder or granular solids before making the solid detergent mushy. More liquid surfactant can usually be blended into a liquid detergent. The liquid detergents commonly contain at least some water to help liquify the other additives and still have the detergent pourable. The liquid detergents may also have other liquids, such as alcohol or a hydrotrope, to help blend all the additives together.

Laundry detergents may have ingredients to help control the pH of the wash water. For example, solid detergents usually contain sodium carbonate (soda ash) or sodium bicarbonate to maintain pH by neutralising any acidic materials that may enter the wash water. Some other ingredients which solid detergents may have include sodium silicate or some form of sodium phosphate such as trisodium orthophosphate, monosodium orthophosphate, or a form of tripolyphosphate. In some locations, phosphate is no longer used as an additive due to environmental concerns.

Some laundry detergents have enzymes to help in stain removal. Some laundry detergents have fabric softeners. Perfume or color ingredients are sometimes added for better smell or to give a detergent some color.

Washing Machine

A washing machine is a machine designed to clean laundry, i.e. clothing and other household textile such as towels and sheets. It is generally restricted to machines that use water as the primary cleaning solution, as opposed to dry cleaning which uses alternative cleaning fluids and is generally performed by specialist businesses.

An early washing machine was constructed in 1767 by Jacob Christian Schäffern. Mechanical washing machines date back to at least the 19th century, and their basic principles of operation have remained largely unchanged. Their first purpose is to suspend the material to be cleaned in water containing detergent. The clothes and water are then "agitated" - moved back and forth repeatedly.

The water is then pumped out and the clothes partially dried by spinning them rapidly in a low-speed centrifuge. Clean water is then added and the clothes and water agitated to remove any remaining traces of the detergent. Finally, the clothes are (usually) spun again (though some clothes are removed immediately and dried by alternative means without further spinning).

Virtually all contemporary washing machines are powered by electricity, though hand-powered or even steam-powered machines were common in earlier times.

They are almost universal in wealthier countries, though some people living in smaller apartments do not have room for them and use communal launderettes.

Automatic washing machines became popular in the 1960s. These automate the washing process by controlling the water and soap intake, draining and rotation of the drum in sequence. Different types of material can be handled by using different programmed cycles. For example, a wool wash needs a low temperature and less agitation than a heavy soil cotton wash.

Most automatic washing machines control the sequence using an electromechanical cam timer, though recently fully electronic systems based on microprocessors have become more widely available. Another approach to programming the wash cycle that was tried was the Hoover Keymatic system, in which plastic cartridges with different key-like profiles were inserted into a slot and read by a mechanical reader. This system was short lived and not terribly successful - the cartridges were prone to getting lost and offered no real advantage over the conventional rotary dial. In hindsight these can be seen as a marketing gimmick rather than a technological breakthrough.

Contemporary washing machines are available in two main configurations: "top loading" and "front loading". The "top loading" design, most popular in the United States, Australia and parts of Europe, places the clothes in a vertically-mounted cylinder, with a propeller-like agitator in the center of the bottom of the cylinder. "Top loading" machines in Asia use impellers instead of agitators. Impellers are similar to agitators except that they don't have the center post extending up in the middle of the wash tub basket.

Clothes are loaded through the top of the machine, which is covered with a hinged door. The "front loading" design, most popular in Europe, instead mounts the cylinder horizontally. Loading is through a glass door at the front of the machine. The cylinder is also called the drum. Agitation is supplied by the back-and-forth rotation of the cylinder, and by gravity. The clothes are lifted up by paddles in the drum and then dropped. This motion flexes the weave of the fabric and forces water and detergent solution through the clothes load. Although more infrequent, there is also a variant of the horizontal axis design that is loaded from the top, through a small door in the circumference of the drum. These machines usually have a shorter cylinder and are therefore smaller.

All washing machines work by using three different sources of energy. They use mechanical energy, thermal energy, and chemical action. Mechanical energy is imparted to the clothes load by the rotation of the agitator in "top loaders", or by the tumbling action of the drum in "front loaders". Thermal energy is supplied by the temperature of the wash bath. Many "front loading" machines have electrical heating elements to heat the wash bath to near boiling.

Chemical action is supplied by the detergent and other laundry chemicals. "Front loaders" use special detergents that are designed to release different chemical ingredients at different temperatures. This is so that different type of stains and soils will be cleaned from the clothes as the wash water is heated up by the electrical heater. "Front loaders" also need to use low sudsing detergents because the tumbling action of the drum folds air into the clothes load that can cause over sudsing.

Tests comparing front-loading and top-loading machines have shown that, in general, front-loaders wash clothes more thoroughly, cause less wear, and use less water and energy than top-loaders. As a result of using less water, they require less detergent to be used, or conversely, they can use the same amount of detergent with less water, which increases detergent concentration and increases the amount of chemical action. They also allow a dryer to be more easily mounted directly above the washer.

Top-loaders do have the advantage in that they complete a washing cycle much faster, tend to cost less for the same capacity machine, and allow clothes to be removed at intermediate stages of the cycle (for instance, if some clothes within a wash are not to be spun). In the late 1990s, the British inventor James Dyson launched a type of washing machine with two cylinders rotating in opposite directions; which, it is claimed, reduces the wash time and produces cleaner results.

Agitator

An agitator is the mechanism in a top load washing machine that projects from the bottom of the wash basket that creates the wash action by rotating back and forth, rolling garments from the top of the load, down to the bottom, then back up again. The following types are known: dual-rollover, dual-action, and triple-rollover action agitators.

Washing /Drying machine

The single appliance can perform both washing and drying functions to cut out the process of loading and unloading clothes from one machine to another. The problem with such machines is that only half of the laundry can be dried after the washing process is complete. Nowadays, some washing/driers are capable of performing both functions in a single machine without interruption and with the full laundry load.

Connectivity

Some modern washing machines include USB or Wifi ports to connect to a domotic network or to the Internet.

Wahs board

The Washboard is a tool designed for hand washing clothing. With mechanised cleaning of clothing becoming more common, by the end of the 20th century the washboard became better known from its originally subsidiary use as a musical instrument.

The traditional washboard is usually constructed with a rectangular wooden frame in which are mounted a series of ridges for the clothing to be rubbed upon. In 19th century washboards the ridges were often of wood as well; in the 20th century ridges of metal became more common. In the late 20th century and early 21st century ridges of galvanised steel are most common. Washboards with brass ridges are still made, and some who use washboards as musical instruments prefer the sound of the somewhat more expensive brass boards.

Though the washboard is generally used as a musical instrument or sound-making device, many parts of the world still use them for washing clothes. In the Southern United States, the washboard has long been a preferred tool for washing soiled clothes. More and more modern laundromat facilities are beginning to offer coin-operated electric washers, but some patrons prefer the washboard as it is much easier to use and significantly cheaper per load of clothes.

The Washboard and Frottoir are used as a percussion instrument, employing the ribbed metal surface of the cleaning device as a rhythm instrument. The washboard is used in many diverse forms of music such as jazz, cajun, jug band and old time music.

The washboard is mounted in a wooden frame while the frottoir is made only from the metal ribbing and is hung around the neck and called the Cajun or Zydeco Rub-Board Vest; this is a late 20th century variation on the washboard designed specifically for musical use. It was, almost certainly, invented by one of Clifton "King of Zydeco" Chenier's associates.

The frottoir or vest frottoir (from Cajun French "vest to be rubbed") is played as a stroked percussion instrument, often in a band with a drummer, while the washboard generally is a replacement for drums. In a jug band, the washboard was stroked with a single whisk-broom and functions as the drums for the band, playing only on the back-beat, for most songs, as a substitute for a snare drum. In a four-beat measure, the washboard will stroke on the 2-beat and the 4-beat. Best sound is achieved using a single steel-wire snare-brush, or whisk-broom.

Clothes Washing

Washing is one way of cleaning, namely with water and often some kind of soap or detergent. Washing is an essential part of good hygiene. Soap assists in the reduction of oils and dirt particles so they can be washed away. People usually wash themselves. Little children and sick and disabled people may be washed by someone else. For fun lovers etc. may wash each other. Often a shower is used, and/or a bathtub. More frequent is washing of just the hands, e.g. before and after preparing food and eating, after using the toilet, after handling something dirty, etc.

Clothes dryer

A clothes dryer or tumble dryer is a major household appliance that is used to remove the residual moisture from clothing or fabrics, generally shortly after being cleaned in a washing or washing/drying machine. Most dryers consist of a rotating drum through which high-temperature air is circulated. The hot air removes the moisture from the fabric through evaporation. The drum is rotated relatively slowly in order to create a tumbling effect. In most cases, the drum is belt-driven by an induction motor. There are generally two classes of dryer: electric and gas. Both of these refer to the method used to elevate the temperature of the air flowing through the drum.

Electric dryers

The electric dryer generally uses a coiled wire that is heated by using electric current. The amount of electric current is varied to adjust the air temperature.

Gas dryers

The gas dryer employs a gas burner that burns natural gas, propane or butane to form a jet of hot gases that are directed into a venturi chamber that uses the bernoulli effect to pull in ambient air so as to raise its temperature. The air temperature can be adjusted by adjusting the size of the gas flame or more commonly by merely switching it on and off.

Condenser dryers

Condenser dryers are ventless and can be either electric or gas. There are two types: water cooled and air cooled. Condenser dryers generally have smaller capacity and longer drying times than vented dryers. Models exist which combine a washing machine and a dryer.

A clothes dryer can be found in just about every house in the United States, and millions more of them are manufactured each year. They are very reliable, and very cheap to build. You'll be surprised at how simple this common machine is. Clothes dryers have:

— A rotating tumbler that holds the clothes.

— An electric or gas powered heater that heats the air that is drawn through the clothes as they tumble, which in turn heats up the clothes and the water in them.

— An exhaust vent that passes out of the dryer and out of the house—this is how the water exits the dryer in the form of steam.

Laundromat

A laundromat (U.S.), launderette (British), Washette (Southeastern U.S.) or washateria (Southwestern U.S.) is a store where clothes are washed and dried. This is often done by coin operated machines that are worked by the client. Laundromats may have a staff to wash the clothing; this is referred to as Fluff-n-Fold or drop-off service. Laundries are equipped with both washing machines and dryers, usually specialised ones designed to survive heavy use.

The washers in many stores are of the front loading variety. The design of the machines uses less water and provides a gentler wash. Capacities of these machines can allow up to 85 pounds of dry weight laundry. In addition, the lower resource consumption of the front loader decreases the impact upon the infrastructures of the community.

Laundromats can have fulltime attendants, part-time or none. Often, you will find the laundries to have a bill changer to facilitate the operation of the machines. Recently, there has been a switch to card operated stores. The laundry will issue a plastic card similar to a credit card which will contain a value which has been pre-paid.

The name laundromat was originally coined by Westinghouse as a trademark for washing machines, however, due to heavy use of the term by others, the phrase is considered to be generic, and has, in all probability, lost trademark status.

Laundry symbols

Laundry symbols, also called care symbols, are pictograms which represent different methods of washing, drying, dry-cleaning and ironing clothing. They are written on labels attached to clothing, to indicate how a particular item should best be cleaned. There are different standards for care labels for the different countries/regions of the world. Below there are links to four of the most common standards. In some standards, pictograms coexist or are complemented by written instructions.The Canadian system is the most colourful one - it uses three colours - green for "go ahead", yellow for "be careful", and red for "stop".

Dry Cleaning

Dry Cleaning is any cleaning process for clothing and textiles using a solvent other than water. Early dry cleaners used petroleum based solvents such as gasoline and kerosene. Concerns over flamability lead William Joseph Stoddard, a dry cleaner from Atlanta, to develop Stoddard solvent as a slightly less flammable alterative to gasoline based solvents. The use of highly flammable petroleum solvents lead to many fires and explosions, which resulted in heavy regulation of dry cleaners.

After World War I dry cleaners began using various chlorinated solvents, because they were much less flamable than petroleum solvents and had much greater cleaning power. By the mid-1930s the dry cleaning industry settled on perchloroethylene (perc) as the ideal solvent. It is stable, nonflammable, and has excellent cleaning power while being gentle to garments.

Process of drycleaning

A dry cleaning machine is somewhat similar to combination of a domestic washing machine, and clothes dryer. Garments are placed into a washing/extraction chamber (refered to as the "basket"). This is the core of the dry cleaning machine. The washing chamber contains a horizontal, perforated drum that rotates within an outer shell. The shell holds the solvent while the rotating drum holds the garment load. Depending on the size of the machine the basket capcity will be between 20 and 80 lb of garments.

During the wash cycle the chamber is filled approximatly 1/3rd full of solvent and begins to rotate to agitate the clothing. The solvent temperature is controlled at 85*F, as a higher temperature may extract dye from the garments causing color loss. During the wash cycle, the chamber is constantly fed a supply of fresh solvent from the working solvent tank while spent solvent is removed and sent to a filter unit. The ideal flow rate is one gallon of solvent per pound of garments per minute.

A typical wash cycle lasts for 8-15 minutes depending on the type of garments and amount of soiling. During the first three minutes solvent-soluble soils disolve into the perchloroethylene and loose insoluble soil from fabrics comes off. It takes approximatly ten to twelve minutes after the loose soil has come off to remove all of the ground-in insoluble soil from the garments. Machines using hydrocarbon solvents require a much longer wash cycle of at least 25 minutes because of the much slower rate of solvation of solvent soluble soils (e.g oily stains).

At the end of wash cycle, the machine starts a rinse cycle and the garmet load is rinsed with fresh distilled solvent from the pure solvent tank. This pure solvent rinse prevents discoloration of garments caused by soil particles being adsorbed back onto the garment surface from the "dirty" working solvent.

After the rinse cycle the machine begins the extraction process. This process recovers dry cleaning solvent for reuse. Modern drycleaning machines can recover approximatly %99.99 of the solvent used in the cleaning process.

The extraction begins by draining the solvent out of the washing chamber cycle and accelerating the basket to speeds of 350 to 450 rpm, causing much of the solvent to spin free of the fabric. When no more solvent can be spun out, the machine starts its drying cycle.

During the drying cycle the garmets are tumbled in continious stream of warm air that circulates through the basket evaporating any traces of solvent left behind after the spin cycle. The temperature of the air is carefully controlled to prevent overdrying and heat damage to the garments. The warm air then passes to through a chiller unit where the solvent vapors are condensed, and returned to the distilled solvent tank. Modern dry cleaning machines use a closed loop system where the chilled air is then reheated and recirculated. This results in very high solvent recovery rates.

After the drying cycle is completed, a deodorizing (aeration) cycle starts to cool the garments and remove the last traces of dry cleaning solvent, by circulating cool outside air over the garments and then through a vapor recovery filter made from activated carbon and polymer resins. At the end of the aeration cycle, the dry cleaned garments are clean, odorless and ready for pressing/ finishing.

Use of solvent

Working solvent from the washing chamber passes through several filtration steps before it it returned to washing chamber. The first step is a button trap which prevents small objects (lint, fasteners, buttons, coins etc) from entering the solvent pump. Next the solvent passes through a filter unit which removes lint and insoluble suspended soils from the solvent. Several different types are used, most filters use an ultra fine mesh to support a thin layer of filter powder (made from diatomaceous earth and activated clays). Some machines use powderless filters which are capable a removing soil particles greater than 30 micrometers from the solvent.

As the machine is used, a thin layer of filter cake (called muck) accumulates on the surface of the lint filter. The muck is removed regularly (once per day) and then further processed to recover any solvent trapped in the muck. Many machines use "spin disc filters" in which the muck is removed from the filter surface by centrifugal action while the filter is backwashed with solvent.

After passing through the lint filter, the solvent passes through an adsorptive cartridge filter, this filter is made from activated clays and charcoal and removes fine insoluble soil and non-volatile residues along with dyes from solvent. Finally the solvent passes through a polishing filter which removes any traces of soil not removed by the previous filters. The clean working solvent is then returned to the working solvent tank.

To enhance cleaning power, small amounts of detergent (0.5%-1.5%) are added to the working solvent and are essential to its functionality. These detergents help disolove hydrophilic soils and keep soil from redepositing on garments. Depending on the machine's design, either an anionic or cationic detergent is used.

Cooked muck

Cooked Powder Residue—The waste material generated by cooking down or distilling muck. Cooked powder residue is a hazardous waste and will contain solvent, powdered filter material (diatomite), carbon, non-volatile residues, lint, dyes, grease, soils and water.

Sludge

The waste sludge or solid residue from the still. Still bottoms contain solvent, water, soils, carbon and other non-volatile residues. Still bottoms from chlorinated solvent drycleaning operations are hazardous wastes.

Environment

Perc is toxic and some believe that long-term exposure can cause liver and kidney damage, though no study has conclusively proven that. There are other solvents that have not been associated with this negative publicity, including:

— Wet cleaning with biodegradable soap and water.

— Silicon and liquid CO_2 solvents.

— Alternative hydrocarbon solvents.

Wet cleaning: This is a system that uses biodegradable soap and water. Computer-controlled dryers and stretching machines ensure that the fabric retains its natural size and shape. Wet cleaning is claimed to purportedly clean 99.9% of "dry clean only" garments safely, including leather; suede; most tailored woolens, silks and rayons.

Silicone and Liquid CO_2 Solvents: Relatively new approaches to dry cleaning have been developed based on both liquid carbon dioxide (usually obtained as a recycled byproduct of other industrial processes) and silicone. Dry cleaners using these solvents are currently few in number.

Alternative Petroleum Solvents: This is more like standard dry cleaning, but the processes use alternative hydrocarbon solvents such as Exxon D-2000 or Chevron-Phillips' EcoSolv. Alternative solvents tend to be much less effective than perc, and very flamable creating a substantial explosion and fire hazard.

Hotel and Motel Laundry Maintaining

Like many companies that are dependent on travellers, The hotel and motel industry has taken a hit. Owners and managers have had to review all areas of expenses and cost, including their linen service. In the case of properties that have on-premise laundries, the laundry department has had to look at saving money with variable costs. The percentages associated with laundry cost are important to know when trying to evaluate cost. All costs are important, but some are bigger than others.

Cost of Labour

Cost of wages and benefits to employees. A manager should review procedures and training in order to optimise the output per employee, commonly referred to as pounds per operator hour. Knowing the productivity of employees, and what it should be for the type of laundry and equipment in use is critical to controlling labour cost.

Cost of Linen Replacement

Cost of replacing linens to a pre-determined par-stock A manger should evaluate the quality and life of linens. This can include theft, normal wear, and intensity of wash formulas, rejects, and overall handling procedures by housekeeping personnel, as well as the laundry staff. Buying the right quality and controlling its use can be beneficial to reducing replacement cost.

Cost of Energy

Cost of water, sewer, electricity, and gas A manager can evaluate equipment efficiency in wash formulas - full loads, proper temperatures, and cycle times—and see that all are balanced to deliver high quality with a low rewash percentage. Properly utilising dryers with full loads, correct temperatures and times helps control finishing costs. This is a variable cost that is often overlooked, but is a real cost that should be analysed closely.

Cost of Chemicals

Cost of all supplies used to clean linens A manager should review all options to take advantage of technology that can deliver the benefits of controlling cost in the above areas as well as the chemistry itself. The chemistry used can dramatically affect other variable cost, so close scrutiny is well advised.

Cost of maintenance, depreciation, equipment, and laundry floor space A manager may be able to help control maintenance by maximising equipment efficiency and using preventive maintenance. Reducing total hours of operation can reduce cost associated with room and space by cutting lighting, heating, or air conditioning cost, etc.

5

Staffing Operations

There are several activities involved in staffing a housekeeping operation. Executive housekeepers must select and interview employees, participate in an orientation programme, train newly hired employees, and develop employees for future growth. Each region has its own demographic situations that affect the availability of suitable employees for involvement in housekeeping or environmental service operations. For example, in one area, an exceptionally high response rate from people seeking food service work may occur and a low response rate from people seeking housekeeping positions may occur.

In another area, the reverse may be true, and people interested in housekeeping work may far outnumber those interested in food service. Advertising campaigns that will reach these employees are the best method of locating suitable people. Major classified ads associated with mass hirings will specify the need for food service personnel, front desk clerks, food servers, housekeeping personnel, and maintenance people. Such ads may yield surprising results.

If aliens are hired, the department manager must take great care to ensure that they are legal residents of this country and that their green cards are valid. More than one hotel department manager has had an entire staff swept away by the Department of Immigration after hiring people who were illegal aliens. Such unfortunate action has required the immediate assistance of all available employees to fill in. Whether you are involved in a mass hiring or in the recruiting of a single employee, a systematic and courteous procedure for processing applicants is essential.

For example, in the opening of the Los Angeles Airport Marriott, 11,000 applicants were processed to fill approximately 850 positions in a period of about two weeks. The magnitude of such an operation required a near assembly-line technique, but a personable and positive experience for the applicants still had to be maintained. The efficient handling of lines of employees, courteous attendance, personal concern for employee desires, and reference to suitable departments for those unfamiliar with what the hotel or hospital has to offer all become earmarks for how the company will treat its employees.

The key to proper handling of applicants is the use of a control system whereby employees are conducted through the steps of application, prescreening, and if qualified, reference to a department for interview. Even though an employee may desire involvement in one classification of work, he or she may be hired for employment in a different department. Also, employees might not be aware of the possibilities available in a particular department at the time of application or may be unable to locate in desired departments at the time of mass hirings. Employees who perform well should therefore be given the opportunity to transfer to other departments when the opportunities arise.

According to laws regulated by federal and state Fair Employment Practices Agencies (FEPA), no person may be denied the opportunity to submit application for employment for a position of his or her choosing. Not only is the law strict on this point, but companies in any way benefiting from interstate commerce may not discriminate in the hiring of people based on race, colour, national origin, or religious preference.

INFORMAL ORIENTATION PROGRAMME

Too often, a new employee is told where the work area and restroom are, given a cursory explanation of the job, then put to work. It is not uncommon to find managers putting employees to work who have not even been processed into the organisation, an unfortunate situation that is usually discovered on payday when there is no paycheck for the new employee. Such blatant disregard for the concerns of the employee can only lead to a poor perception of the company.

A planned orientation programme will eliminate this type of activity and will bring the employee into the company with personal concern and with a greater possibility for a successful relationship. A good orientation programme is usually made up of four phases: employee acquisition, receipt of an employee's handbook, tour of the facility, and an orientation meeting.

Employee Acquisition: Once a person is accepted for employment, the applicant is told to report for work at a given time and place, and that place should be the personnel department. Pre-employment procedures can take as much as one-half day, and department managers eager to start new employees to work should allow time for a proper employee acquisition into the organisation. At this time it should be ensured that the application is complete and any additional information pertaining to employment history that may be necessary to obtain the necessary work permits and credentials is on hand.

Usually the security department records the entry of a new employee into the staff and provides instructions regarding use of employee entrances, removing parcels from the premises, and employee parking areas. Application for work permits, and drug testing, will be scheduled where applicable. All documents required by the hotel's health and welfare insurer should be completed, and instructions should be given about immediately reporting accidents, no matter how slight, to supervisors.

Familiarisation of Facilities: Upon completion of the acquisition phase, a facility tour should be conducted for one or all new employees. For new facilities, access to the property should be gained within about one week before opening, and many new employees can be taken on a tour simultaneously. It is possible for employees to work in the hotel housekeeping department for years and never to have visited the showroom, dining rooms, ballrooms, or even the executive office areas.

A tour of the complete facility melds employees into the total organisation, and a complete informative tour should never be neglected. For ongoing operations, after acquisition, the new employee may be turned over to a department supervisor, who becomes the tour director. An appreciation of the total involvement of each employee is strengthened when a facilities tour is complete and thorough.

Employee Orientation Meeting

Employee orientation meetings that are scheduled too soon fail to answer many questions that will develop within the first two weeks of employment. The meeting should be held in a comfortable setting, with refreshments provided. It is usually conducted by the director of human resources and is attended by as many of the facility managers as possible. Most certainly, the general manager or hospital administration members of the executive committee, the security director, and the new employees' department heads should attend. Each of these managers should have an opportunity to welcome the new employees and give them a chance to associate names with faces.

All managers and new employees should wear name tags. In orientation meetings, a brief history of the company and company goals should be presented. Although the new employee will be gaining confidence and security in the position as training ends and work is actually performed, informal orientation may continue for quite some time. The formal orientation, however, ends with the orientation meeting. Finally, it should be remembered that good orientation procedures lead to worker satisfaction and help quiet the anxieties and fears that a new employee may have.

Quality of Training

Such ability will depend in part on past experiences, but more commonly it can be credited to the type and quality of training offered. Employees, regardless of past experiences, always need some degree of training before starting a new job. Small institutions may try to avoid training by hiring people who are already trained in the general functions with which they will be involved. However, most institutions recognise the need for training that is specifically oriented toward the new experience, and will have a documented training programme.

Some employers of housekeeping personnel find it easier to train completely unskilled and untrained personnel. In such cases, bad or undesirable practices do not have to be trained out of an employee. Previous experience and education should, however, be analysed and considered in the training of each new employee in order that efficiencies in training can be recognised. If an understanding of department standards and policies can be demonstrated by a new employee, that portion of training may be shortened or modified. However, skill and ability must be demonstrated before training can be altered.

First training of a new employee actually starts with a continuation of department orientation. When a new employee is turned over to the housekeeping or environmental services department, orientation usually continues by familiarising the employee with department rules and regulations. Many housekeeping departments have their own department employee handbooks.

Training may be defined as those activities that are designed to help an employee begin performing tasks for which he or she is hired or to help the employee improve performance in a job already assigned. The purpose of training is to enable an employee to begin an assigned job or to improve upon techniques already in use. In hotel or hospital housekeeping operations, there are three basic areas in which training activity should take place: skills, attitudes, and knowledge.

Employees need guidance in their attitudes about the work that must be done. They need to be guided in their thinking about rooms that may present a unique problem in cleaning. Attitudes among section housekeepers need to be such that, occasionally, when rooms require extra effort to be brought back to standard, it is viewed as being a part of rendering service to the guest who paid to enjoy the room. The rooms are there to be enjoyed. Positive relationships with various agencies and people also need to be developed.

The most important task of the trainer is to prepare new employees to meet standards. With this aim in mind, sequence of performance in cleaning a guestroom is most important in order that efficiency in accomplishing day-to-day tasks may be developed. In addition, the best method of accomplishing a task should be presented to the new trainee.

New equipment may require new attitudes about work habits. Employee behaviour while on the job that is seen as an indicator for additional training may be divided into two categories: events that the manager witnesses and events that the manager is told about by the employees. Events that the manager witnesses that indicate a need for training are frequent employee absence, considerable spoilage of products, carelessness, a high rate of accidents, and resisting direction by supervisors. Events that the manager might be told about that indicate a need for training are that something doesn't work right, something is dangerous to work with, something is making work harder.

Although training is vital for any organisation to function at top efficiency, it is expensive. The money and man-hours expended must therefore be worth the investment. There must be a balance between the dollars spent training employees and the benefits of productivity and high-efficiency performance. A simple method of determining the need for training is to measure performance of workers: Find out what is going on at present on the job, and match this performance with what should be happening.

The difference, if any, describes how much training is needed. If the employee could not do the job even if his or her life depended on the outcome, there is a deficiency of knowledge (DK). If the employee could have done the job if his or her life depended on the outcome, but did not, there is a deficiency of execution (DE). If either deficiency of knowledge or deficiency of execution exists, training must be conducted. The approach or the method of training may differ, however. Deficiencies of knowledge can be corrected by training the employee to do the job, then observing and correcting as necessary until the task is proficiently performed.

Methods of Training

Each method has its own advantages and disadvantages, which must be weighed in the light of benefits to be gained. Some methods are more expensive than others but are also more effective in terms of time required for comprehension and proficiency that must be developed. Several useful methods of training housekeeping personnel are listed and discussed.

On-the-Job Training

Using on-the-job training (OJT), a technique in which "learning by doing" is the advantage, the instructor demonstrates the procedure and then watches the students perform it. With this technique, one instructor can handle several students. In housekeeping operations, the instructor is usually a GRA who is doing the instructing in the rooms that have been assigned for cleaning that day. The OJT method is not operationally productive until the student is proficient enough in the training tasks to absorb part of the operational load.

Simulation Training

With simulation training, a model room (unrented) is set up and used to train several employees. Whereas OJT requires progress toward daily production of ready rooms, simulation requires that the model room not be rented. In addition, the trainer is not productive in cleaning ready rooms. The advantages of simulation training are that it allows the training process to be stopped, discussed, and repeated if necessary. Simulation is an excellent method, provided the trainer's time is paid for out of training funds, and clean room production is not necessary during the workday.

Coach-Pupil Method

The coach-pupil method is similar to OJT except that each instructor has only one student (a one-to-one relationship). This method is desired, provided that there are enough qualified instructors to have several training units in progress at the same time.

Lectures

The lecture method reaches the largest number of students per instructor. Practically all training programmes use this type of instruction for certain segments. Unfortunately, the lecture method can be the dullest training technique, and therefore requires instructors who are gifted in presentation capabilities. In addition, space for lectures may be difficult to obtain and may require special facilities.

Conferences

The conference method of instruction is often referred to as workshop training. This technique involves a group of students who formulate ideas, do problem solving, and report on projects. The conference or workshop technique is excellent for supervisory training.

Demonstrations

When new products or equipment are being introduced, demonstrations are excellent. Many demonstrations may be conducted by vendors and purveyors as a part of the sale of equipment and products. Difficulties may arise when language barriers exist. It is also important that no more information be presented than can be absorbed in a reasonable period of time; otherwise misunderstandings may arise.

Whereas training begins after orientation of an employee who is hired to do a specific job, upon introduction of new equipment, or upon observation and communication with employees indicating a need for training, development begins with the identification of a specific employee who has shown potential for advancement. Training for promotion or to improve potential is in fact development and must always include a much neglected type of training -supervisory training. Many forms of developmental training may be given on the property; other forms might include sending candidates to schools and seminars.

Developmental training is associated primarily with supervisors and managerial development and may encompass many types of experiences. Development of individuals within the organisation looks to future potential and promotion of employees. Specifically, those employees who demonstrate leadership potential should be developed through supervisory training for advancement to positions of greater responsibility. Unfortunately, many outstanding workers have their performance rewarded by promotion but are given no development training. The excellent section housekeeper who is advanced to the position of senior housekeeper without the benefit of supervisory training is quickly seen to be unhappy and frustrated and may possibly become a loss to the department.

Development of new growth in the trainee becomes difficult when the training instructor or coordinator is not only developing a new manager but is also being held responsible for the production of some aspect of housekeeping operations. Whether you are conducting a training or a development programme, suitable records of training progress should be maintained both by the training supervisor and the student. Periodic evaluations of the student's progress should be conducted, and successful completion of the programme should be recognised. Public recognition of achievement will inspire the newly trained or developed employee to achieve standards of performance and to strive for advancement.

Future performance may be based on beginning performance after training. If an employee's performance begins to fall short of standards and expectations, there has to be a reason other than lack of skills. The reason for unsatisfactory performance must then be sought out and addressed. This type of follow-up is not possible unless suitable records of training and development are maintained and used for comparison. Although evaluation and performance appraisal for employees will occur as work progresses, it is not uncommon to find the design of systems for appraisal as part of organisation and staffing functions.

6

Employee Recognition and Motivation

The foundation of recognition and motivation is that people need and want Acceptance, Approval and Appreciation. Almost all positive motivation is based on these needs. People want to know that what they do makes a difference. Just recognizing the staff is the most important step one can take. The labour market where your hotel, restaurant or resort is located is undoubtedly difficult and unique. Nobody really understands how difficult it is to staff your business with an adequate number of competent, caring, efficient, and trustworthy, employees.

Interestingly, the hotel managers who complained of staffing difficulties had high turnover of new employees. The hotels with low turnover didn't feel there were staffing problems. Further, there was no correlation to hotels with staffing problems and any objectively quantifiable socioeconomic issues in the surrounding communities. Interviews with regional supervisors at other hotel companies revealed that they had the same situation but not necessarily in the same communities.

Any time an employee quits or is terminated the supervisor and manager should ask themselves these three questions:

1. Should the person have been hired in the first place? Adequate screening depends on the obvious interview questions as well as the not-so-obvious but still legal ones. Why do you want this particular job, how will you get to work, what other kinds of jobs have you been applying for? To the greatest extent possible, require that all applicants pass job-related skills testing and examine the person's ability to follow directions and learn. Don't hire someone just because you are desperate without taking the time to check references and in some cases credit and criminal records. You do have a release on your employment application, don't you?
2. Did the employee receive an adequate orientation and quality training? Did anyone that cared explain the mission, culture, physical layout, rules, etc. of the hotel or restaurant? Did he or she meet other employees and leaders during a tour of the hotel? All those things are part of an orientation and give a new employee an even playing field to start with so they are familiar with the workplace and feel as if they belong. Training should be conducted by supervisors and staff who are trained to train, have lesson plans, and understand the learning process. Is it fair to a new employee to have them trained by someone who isn't even good at the job, is overworked, and is not certifiably enthusiastic about their job and the business?
3. Did the employee benefit from good leadership? Leadership is a balance of positive and negative incentives specifically tailored to the individual and the circumstances. A public praising for some employees might be more effective than a raise while a thank you note or a pat on the back will be enough

for another. As to negative incentives, it is essential that they be implemented in a timely and constructive manner. Further, the severity of negative feedback must be tailored to the individual and the undesired behaviour or work quality. All negative feedback should have a positive goal where everyone and the business gains rather than simply punishment.

If these questions are reviewed whenever an employee leaves for whatever reason, management should be able to improve their ability to handle each of these three items. The result will be lower turnover which will save the business money, make it a more desirable workplace for all, and provide the guest and patron with consistent, quality service.

A few other thoughts are in order regarding recruiting.

— Good employees are like alcoholics, they hang around with like-minded people. Get current employees to help recruit new staff and reward them with cash after an agreed-upon retention period, it works.

— There is nothing wrong with recruiting good people you observe in other hotels and businesses.

— Advertise for job openings in non-traditional areas of the classifieds. Only out-of-work hotel and restaurant workers look under hotels and restaurants.

Creative Recruiting

The Creative Recruiting sessions were built around the Educational Institute (E.I.) of the American Hotel & Motel Association's (AH&MA) video and other materials by the same name. While these materials do not have all the answers they are an excellent start. It was clear that in addition to doing the traditional things needed to do more. An idea which surfaced as one with great potential was inviting people in retail, fast food and other businesses who were observed to be the kind of employee we wanted to come in for an interview and get acquainted. It was generally agreed that doing that to your competitors would be damaging in the long run and that there were plenty of other industries to recruit among.

Interviewing and Hiring

While on the surface one might have thought the materials did not always apply to interviewing room attendants, the fact is the materials did not always apply to improving one's interviewing and hiring skills at all levels. Following are the reasons of why interviews fail. The interviewer

- Fails to gain enough information by running out of time or questions.
- Does not match the candidate with the job because he does not understand the true job description.
- Fails to evaluate the resume by overlooking key factors that could provide information about the candidate.
- Settles for a superficial, rehearsed answer by not probing past the answers for additional information.
- Is only concerned with skills rather than personality.

Train the Trainer

In many hotels they use all three methods covered by these videos, particularly video.

Customer Service

This programme started with identifying customers, both internal and external to the operation. Subsequently, time was spent on people's perceptions and expectations. In doing business with your organization, customers have many points of contact and at each point have a chance to form an impression. These impressions are generally good or bad. Negative examples include long waiting lines, faded signs, dirty surroundings, and forgotten promises. Positive examples include attention to details, friendliness, ownership of problems, quick solutions and clean neat surroundings.

The following list helped us focus on who we should be recruiting because most of these are not items that can be trained into people:

— Motivated to Serve.
— Sincerely interested in others
— Positive Attitude
— Energized and enthusiastic
— They take initiative
— They know the organization

A couple of anecdotes: Near our corporate office there is a jewellery store. It is a modern, well designed facility with good signage and attractive display cases. Lots of glass, special microscopes, private viewing rooms, etc. A piece of tape holds a faded, hand lettered sheet of paper under the attractive brass plate with the store's name on it on the door. The sign says, "Recording devices not permitted on these premises."

Training Sources

With the tremendous growth of the lodging industry over the last two decades, the industry's ability to develop competent management staff has been severely strained. The educational facilities that focus on the industry, whether they are four-year or two-year programmes, cannot keep up with the growth rate and never have been a major contributor of entry level management. The most significant source of the future leaders are line level employees or people moving into this industry from others. This means that company training programmes and OJT (on the job training) are really our keys to developing managers with technical and leadership skills that will contribute to the success of the organization.

Informal Mentoring

Regardless of the source of the emerging managers, they need some support and nurturing to be all they can be. Mentoring is one way to do this. Many of us are familiar with informal mentoring but formal programmes can accomplish much more. Mentor and protege relationships generally occur on an informal basis in the hotel industry. This is typified by the general manager who takes a junior manager under his protective wing and grooms him for greater responsibility.

The traditional mentoring relationship is based on an unspoken agreement and is subject to the availability and good will of the senior manager. Unlike the traditional mentoring relationship, a structured mentoring programme clearly defines the mentoring relationship by ensuring that the mentor, protege, and organization all clearly understand what to expect and what is expected of them. Its goals are the same but its process is different.

Aims of Mentoring

Mentoring, in its traditional or structured form, aims to accomplish the same thing-the pairing of a skilled and experienced senior person (the mentor) with a less experienced and junior person (the protege) to help the protege grow and develop under the guidance of the mentor. The roles that the mentor may play are those of the teacher, supporter or sponsor. As a teacher, the mentor teaches the protege the skills and knowledge needed to perform the job and provides inside information about the organization, such as politics and personalities.

The role of supporter is one in which the mentor helps the protege deal with his career and personal conflicts and pressures, and helps build his self-confidence. And, as a sponsor, the mentor intervenes on the protege's behalf in conflicts that might endanger the protege's career and markets the protege to upper management. Although mentoring provides an attractive training and development alternative, it may not be right for your hotel. Mentoring programmes work best when specific human resource needs and conditions exist. In the absence of these conditions, a mentoring programme could actually hurt rather than help your hotel.

Some basic questions need to be answered before launching a mentoring programme.

— Does your organization need to prepare people within the organization to fill future management positions? Proteges join a mentoring programme with the implicit promise that excellent performance will be rewarded by career advancement. If there is no room at the top for successful proteges, the organization will be burdened with a surplus of ambitious, overqualified, and frustrated individuals who will eventually take their skills and talents elsewhere.

— If future human resource needs are forecasted, are they continuing or one-time needs?

— Does your organization represent an expanding chain of hotels where continued growth insures an on-going need for upper level managers, or does your organization represent a single hotel dealing with attrition-related human resource needs? If this is an infrequent, one-shot occurrence, then a structured mentoring programme would not be cost-effective.

— Does your corporate culture value the veteran employee or does it prefer to buy "new blood" from outside the organization? Developing talent from within the organization takes time, resources, and long-term commitment from upper management, making their support vital to the success of the programme. A high level of upper management interest and commitment is needed from the outset since mentors come from the upper management ranks.

— Does your organization have enough suitable managers available to pair with proteges? Mentors should be at least two position levels above the protege (to prevent mentors from feeling threatened by their proteges), competent, widely respected, secure in their jobs, skilled coaches, and possess excellent interpersonal skills. They should have the time and the willingness to volunteer for the job.

— How will a mentoring programme fit in with your other human resource programmes? If successful succession planning and management development programmes are already in place, will a mentoring programme replicate, replace or enhance it? How will a mentoring programme link to other training programmes? Is there someone who can initiate and oversee the programme? A successful mentoring programme requires someone to coordinate the selection and pairing of mentors and proteges, establish orientation programmes, perform periodic reviews of the pairs, and to help conclude the relationship.

No Panacea

Mentoring is not a panacea for all organizations; however, given the right conditions, its organizational benefits can be enormous. Good mentoring programmes attract the best candidates for a job, reduce turnover of talented people, help people achieve their optimum potential and productivity, assure a smooth transfer of leadership from one generation to the next, and encourage communication up and down the organizational hierarchy.

Implementation Steps

Implementing a mentoring programme requires the same careful planning, implementing, monitoring, and evaluating that any major project requires.

1. *Select mentoring programme coordinator.* The coordinator will be responsible for helping the mentor and protege negotiate an agreement, conduct orientations, monitor the relationship, and assist with concluding the relationship.
2. *Select proteges.* They should be intelligent, ambitious, committed to the organization, have good interpersonal skills, be positively perceived by the organization, and be willing and able to accept greater responsibility.
3. *Determine the developmental needs of the protege.* This can be accomplished by reviewing the protege's work record, interviewing the protege and his manager, and testing.
4. *Select mentors.* They should be technically competent, supported by peers and upper management, have power within the organization, be highly regarded in the organization, feel secure in their positions, have the time and the desire to assume responsibility for a protege's career development, and be able to teach, coach, and motivate others.
5. *Pair proteges and mentors.* Considerations in the paring would be the developmental needs of the protege and

the skills and knowledge of the mentor as well as the personalities of the individuals involved.

6. *Familiarize mentors and proteges with their roles.* Subjects that should be addressed are time commitments, expectations of mentors and proteges, available resources, relationships between mentor, protege, protege's manager, and the mentoring coordinator, and the benefits of mentoring to the mentor, protege, and organization.
7. *Mentors and proteges negotiate and agreement.* Mentors and proteges negotiate an agreement which includes their expectations and responsibilities, confidentiality, duration of the relationship, scheduling of meetings, and the amount of time that will be spent on mentoring activities.
8. *Develop plan.* The mentor and protege develop a plan for meeting the needs of the protege.
9. *Implement plan.* The mentor and protege meet periodically for coaching sessions, evaluating progress, and reviewing the development plan. Progress is periodically reported to the coordinator.
10. *Conclude the relationship.* Relationships might be concluded when all goals are achieved, the agreement date is reached, or the protege and mentor feel that the relationship is no longer productive.

Don't be confused; a mentoring programme might consist of just two or three pairs of people. Whether you undertake a formal mentoring programme as simply take some of these ideas and improve the informal mentoring already occurring in your lodging facility, the result will be a stronger base of people. One of the most surprising results may be improved retention among your entry level managers and the line staff that works for them.

Staff Scheduling and Minimizing

Payroll and related expenses are, in most cases, a hotel's largest expense category. Orientation and training are important. Good leadership, a personalized balance of positive and negative feed back and incentives, are also crucial. Employees are not mind-readers so the orientation, training and leadership are crucial to you and the employee's success. Doing this efficiently consists of several steps. These include:

— Establishing and quantifying your service and productivity standards. This step consists of deciding, for example, how many minutes, on average, it should take to clean a room or how many covers a banquet server is expected to handle for various types of meal service.

— Turning your service and productivity standards into staffing guides. Staffing guides are worksheets which can be used in conjunction with forecasts to establish how many labour hours and/or persons will be necessary to service the expected volume of business over a particular time period in a particular food and beverage (F.& B.) outlet or in the rooms department at the Front Desk, Reservations, Housekeeping, etc.

— Developing forecasting models for the various parts of your business in which volume varies. Generally, these forecasting models should result in forecasts of volume in units, such as covers or rooms broken down into arrivals, stay-overs and checkouts. Exceptions might include sales volume in beverage outlets and reservations calls.

— On a weekly basis, upcoming business volume should be forecasted. Variances between the forecasted business volume and budgeted volume should be clearly understood. If they are negative, both marketing and expense control plans are needed to counteract the impact of the revenue shortfalls. Remember, the best forecasts are made of many little estimates rather than one or two big guesses!

— The forecasts should be applied to the staffing guides to develop staff schedules. Staff schedules should always be costed out and compared to the payroll budgets for the various department. Again, variances need to be studied and understood. In addition to changes in volume, variances can be the result of bad budgeting, poor staffing guides or bad math!

There are also situations where it may be appropriate to charge guests for extra labour they require. The simplest example of this is where a catering patron requests and signs a clear contract for one set-up and then requests a change after the room is set. Depending on the circumstances, including both the importance, as measured in profit potential of the patron and the hotel's circumstances, a fee may be charged for the resetting expense incurred by the hotel.

As a not too minor point, it should be kept in mind that workers' compensation and unemployment insurance expenses are manageable expenses. Pursuing an expense management programme for these two items will, in time, result in reduced payroll burden. The key in these categories, like anything else in payroll expense management, is to be proactive rather than reactive. It may be tough to judge yourself as it relates to payroll and related expenses. All hotels do not have the same resources available for employee benefits.

7

Hotel Protection and Security Management

Hotel protection management consists of an integrated management model and series of approaches which, when properly applied, allow for the establishment and maintenance of an acceptable level of protection. And at the same time the image of hospitality is maintained. Travellers not only do have virtually an unlimited choice of means of travel, but also have an exceptionally broad choice of accommodations when they reach their destination. From casino resorts to private clubs, the traveller has never had such a selection from which to choose.

Further, the traveller can avail himself of a property which functions as a multi-operation facility, at the same time offering long-term accommodations to some (an apartment), both room and food to others (a boarding house), and finally supplying the basic needs of an overnight guest (a traditional hotel.) For all practical purposes, there is little legal difference between any of these types of facilities when it comes to hotel protection management.

The legal definition of inns and hotels can be traced to several legal decisions dating from the late 16th century.

These early legal definitions vary to such a degree that it is difficult for a lay person to derive a common definition. It denies hotel as a house which is held out to the public as a place where all transient persons who come will be received and entertained as guests for business, with food and lodging while on their journey; or a house where travellers are furnished with everything which they have occasion for while upon their way; or a place where transient guests are admitted to lodge, as well as one where they are fed and lodged. Further, the terms innkeeper, hotel-keeper, and hotelier are used interchangeably.

Likewise, the term motel, for all practical purposes, may be used as synonymous with hotel and inn. For the purposes of this text, we should consider all these various forms of accommodations as hotel. Lodging managers have been besieged with a multiplicity of terms which seem to surround the subject of guest protection. These terms, in and of themselves, seem ill-defined, perhaps non-defined, and certainly confusing.

The hotel industry is well advised to adopt a single, descriptive and extremely useful term protection to replace all the ill-defined terms used above. Protection is defined as the state of being protected—the covering or shielding from harm, injury or destruction. Shielding from harm seems to imply that the acts of protecting must, by definition, be proactive. If one is shielded from harm, then it seems evident that the harm will not be allowed to reach the person being protected. A barrier, or protective shield, or line of defence has been established which decreases the possibility and probability of the danger ever reaching and harming or causing loss to the one being protected.

Such action does not prevent the loss by attacking the potential doer of the harm. Rather, by surrounding the intended victim of the harm, it has the effect of reducing the possibility of the harm being inflicted. It does not, in the case of the threat of crime, claim to prevent. Rather it aims to deter the criminal act from ever reaching the target victim. By definition, by design, and by necessity, protection is proactive. As such, the shield or barrier or protective techniques which act as the deterrent must be in place prior to the threat ever occurring. As it is proactive rather than reactive so it differs from the traditional role of the police.

Police devote an extraordinary amount of time to an event after it occurs. We in the private sector must do just the opposite. We must provide protection, not simply what is considered security, before the event occurs. The term security can be a problem in and of itself, and its usefulness as the term to define protection may have run its course. The term causes a mis-focus and should not be used in a modern proactive, management-science-based property protection programme. There are several reasons for this assertion, not the least of which is the fact that the term security conjures visions of a security officer, private police or a security department.

The responsibility of guest protection is limited to those security individuals and security departments, and worse yet, that such care is their exclusive responsibility. Hotel management is art of managing, directing, facilitating or ascertaining the successful accomplishment of tasks or the attainment of stated objectives. In its simplest form management can best be described as that discipline designed and used to get tasks accomplished.

In Hotels, your security is generally based on how the fire is handled. However, many people do not know, or follow, correct procedures in coping with a fire. This is another step you, as a traveller, can take to protect yourself and your family. By choosing a secure hotel, you're choosing a well made, fire-resistant property.

However, many hotels abroad are not as fire-resistant as those here: it may be difficult to contact a fire department; there may not be reliable smoke detectors or sprinkler systems; there may be too few exits and escape routes may not be posted; escape routes may not be posted in hallways; and, fire-fighting equipment and water supplies may be limited. Experts tell us that if a fire starts, try to call the fire department or the police for help—do not rely on a security guard. If you speak the language, tell the fire department or police your room number.

If you cannot reach the fire department, call the front desk—tell them your room number. Grab your key and crawl to the door on your hands and knees. Don't stand—smoke gases rise while the fresher air will be near the floor. Before you open the door, feel it with the palm of your hand. If the door or knob is hot, the fire may be right outside. Open the door slowly. If your exit path is clear, crawl into the hallway. Be sure to close the door behind you to keep smoke out in case you need to return to your room. Take your key as most hotel doors lock automatically. Stay close to the wall to avoid being trampled.

Firefighters remind us to not use elevators during a fire. They may malfunction, or if they have heat-activated call buttons, they may take you directly to the fire floor. They recommend that as you make your way to the fire exit, stay on the same side as the exit door. Count the doors to the exit. Follow the plan that you organised. When you reach the exit, walk down the stairs to the first floor. If you encounter heavy smoke in the stairwell, don't try to run through it. You may not make it. Instead, turn around and walk up to the roof fire exit.

If all exits are blocked, or if there is heavy smoke in the hallway, you'll be better off staying in your room, according to the Fire Department. If there is smoke in your room, open a window and turn on the bathroom vent. Don't break the window unless it can't be opened. You might want to close the window later to keep smoke out, and broken glass could injure you or people below. Fill the bathtub with water to use for fire fighting. Bail water onto your door or any hot walls with an ice bucket or wastebasket. Stuff wet towels into cracks under and around doors where smoke can enter.

Tie a wet towel over your mouth and nose to help filter out smoke. If there is fire outside your window, take down the drapes and move everything combustible away from the window. Emergency evacuation is a part of Hotel Security Procedures. It is especially relevant in high-risk countries. Move directly, without delay or hesitation, on the predetermined escape route. Consider airport security conditions and proceed accordingly. If the airport is expected to be unsafe use alternative means of transport.

Hotel rooms are not safe places for discussions of confidential business matters or classified information. Hotels in certain countries invariably put business visitors in designated rooms, presumably for ease of eavesdropping. Use the hotel to practise your communication skills when travelling abroad. Hotel security also involves effectively utilising hotel personnel as resources for information. Inevitably this includes asking for directions. There is an effective or right way, and an ineffective or wrong way to get directions. The most useful tool for getting or giving directions is a map. Be sure to have one with you when you ask for help.

Challenges

In some instances, when the risks of crime are known to exist, additional security has been recognised as fundamental under the circumstances. In these cases, courts have often held that the following elements are required as a matter of law: track bars for sliding glass doors, closed circuit television, and security guard personnel. Very often hotel chains have corporate security departments consisting of only a few people. This generally happens not because the company ignores its security needs, but because the security employees are assigned as staff to various corporate facilities. So while dozens or even hundreds of people may have a full-time or part-time security function, the corporate staff is limited.

Each facility staff member should have a specifically assigned role to play in the security programme. From housekeeping and maintenance to front desk and executive management staff, everyone should be trained and encouraged to participate in security programmes. Special areas that require total participation of the staff include: general disorders and bomb threats, fire emergencies, overall surveillance, first aid response, maintenance checks, parking lot patrols, response to calls for assistance, record keeping, eyewitness testimony, and internal security.

Different regulations of the country govern the employment of police personnel in private security assignments. In addition, civil liberty issues and conflict of interest possibilities may also be considered in the decision to utilise off-duty police. The hotel should employ any technology it acquires to its full capacity. The reason for this is, that by purchasing it, the hotel is both acknowledging the need for the system, and advising the guests that they are under the protection of the equipment in place.

In the event of loss or injury, that might have been prevented if the installed equipment had been working to its full capacity, the hotel-owner has more claim to defend against. Close circuit television can be an effective security tool when installed and used properly. It should be placed in areas with the greatest likelihood of effective use. Generally remote areas, such as parking lots need coverage, because other eyes and ears are not available for security purposes. Electronic door locks are useful to gain better control over room access problems.

Maintaining adequate key control has long been a vexing problem. Mini-safes have become useful because theft from guest-rooms are responsible for the greatest percentage of reported hotel-related crimes. Maintaining adequate insurance against claims of negligent security is essential both to defend against claims and to pay damages if awarded. Not utilising an investment in security equipment can be as bad or worse than not making the investment at all.

The development of a clearly defined procedural manual is the backbone of the security programme. The procedures manual not only directs the security effort, but also serves as evidence that security considerations have been carefully and logically thought out. Good lighting is an important crime deterrent and prevention tool. In an environment of increasing all-round crime, increased crime in hotel-related matters is not a matter of surprise. Hotels in particular are looked at as targets for local criminals, who see a fertile source of victims carrying cash and valuables. It is common to find criminal elements from adjacent neighbourhoods or those who are even willing to travel relatively long distances for the promise of a good haul from unsuspecting victims.

Certain categories of guests require special security consideration because of behaviour-patterns, special needs, cultural differences or other characteristics that cause security problems to develop. These individuals and groups require special attention to ensure that their stays do not result in preventable losses or injuries to themselves or others. Foreign visitors are often victimised by criminals because they are tricked or misled into placing trust in dangerous individuals or bad advice.

Women travelling on business now represent 40 per cent of business travellers. These women often travelling alone, and have in recent years become the victims of especially brutal crimes including assault, rape and murder. Care should be given with room assignments, and every effort should be made to place women on notice of foreseeable risks. Airline flight crews, and particularly female members of these crews, have been identified by criminals as targets because the regular patterns of their stay is so easy to identify. Room thefts and personal assaults are higher than average for these crews. Student groups, especially those attending proms or other school functions, often lack adequate supervision to ensure that they conform to rules and procedures.

Trade shows, especially catering to industries involved in valuables such as jewellery, furs and electronics, attract thieves from all over the world. Group tours, because of their scheduled departures and the practice of leaving luggage and purchase in lobbies, storage rooms and unattended guest-rooms, suffer a high incidence of loss. Celebrity guests, especially entertainment groups or sports teams, regularly suffer attempts by fans, curious, and persons with criminal intent, to accost them in public spaces, on sidewalks around the hotel, and even in their rooms.

Many hotels have a "dry room" where you can put your luggage and freshen up. If the hotel has more than one building, request a room in or near the main building. Request a room that faces inward towards other rooms or towards the lobby. Request a room that does not have easy access to the window, such as from the roof or street. Request a room on the second floor, but not higher than the seventh floor, near a fire exit, away from stairwells, elevators, ice machines, basements or garbage/refuse rooms. A room near the elevator helps avoid long walks down stairways. If you have valuables or important documents, e.g., passport or airline ticket, store them in the safety deposit box at the front office and get a receipt. Use a room safe to store only items of moderate value.

Large sums of jewellery or money should be placed in the safe at the front desk. If there is no room safe, put valuables in a money belt that you may wear, or bring along a "portable safe". These come in many forms: hollow books, shows with hollow heels, suitcases with hollow compartments, etc. Always use the deadbolt lock when in your room. Always use the chain lock which should be securely fastened to the wall and a solid core door. Windows should open and close easily from the inside.

If you are expecting someone, pre-arrange an exact time of arrival, as well as some form of introduction or identification: a secret knock, business card under the door, or a phone call from the lobby. Completely close the curtains, especially in the evening or if you will be away from the room for sometime. Public announcements are a means to disseminate information about terrorist threats and other relatively short-term and/or transnational conditions posing significant risks to the security of American travellers. They are made any time there is a perceived threat and usually have Americans as a particular target group.

In the past, public announcements have been issued to deal with short-term coups, bomb threats to airlines, violence by terrorists and anniversary dates of specific terrorist events. There are generally, no established and specific 'security' standards within the lodging industry. Each property is unique unto itself—each has different threats and different assets. A property protection programme should be developed so that the selected countermeasures can be appropriate to protect these unique assets against the unique threats.

Access control is that countermeasure designed to limit, monitor, control or otherwise influence the movement of persons and vehicles onto, from, and within a property. Access control is designed to limit access. A locked or otherwise secured door to a storage shed limits access. Ease of access is lessened while not absolutely preventing the unauthorised entry into that building or room. Access control is designed to monitor access. A log-in sheet at a food-storage area monitors the unauthorised entry into that room.

The controlling quality access control is designed to control access. An electronic access code used in conjunction with a touch pad to a restricted area controls the unauthorised entry into that area. Access control is designed to otherwise influence access and the movement of people or vehicles. Perhaps the most obvious example of such successful influencing is the simple use of gender signs on restroom doors. It is obvious then from these and other examples that access control is a relative countermeasure. It is also complementary. That is to say, its effectiveness can be enhanced by its use in concert with other countermeasures and by adjusting the control features with the countermeasure itself.

While locking or otherwise securing the door of a storage shed provides a certain level of protection, the requirement that a roving protection officer intermittently check the building increases the access control protection level. While the requirement that a person entering a restricted food storage area sign in and out, the addition of a time-lapse camera which records such entries obviously makes the access control stronger. The protective features of having an electronic touch pad access to a severely restricted area can be further increased, for instance, by frequent and well-monitored changes to the access code. The example of the gender signs on restrooms is an excellent illustration of how specific access control techniques can overtly influence those whom we are trying to affect. Access control attempts to limit, monitor, control and otherwise influence the movement onto, from and within a property of pedestrian and vehicular traffic.

Many techniques and methods may be utilised successfully in this endeavour. Again, as is the case of all countermeasures, access control is property-specific and the methods and techniques utilised must be similarly individualised. Access control of vehicular traffic begins at the entrance or entrances to the property. In the case of those properties which are located away from and out of sight of the main thoroughfares, access control sometimes begins off the property.

In most instances, with the exception of exclusive resort properties, the entrances to the property are unmonitored. Signs are the most used access control devices at these points. Many properties post signs at the perimeter vehicular access points which enthusiastically welcome guests, and direct vendors. At the same time, these signs discourage unauthorised entrance. Guests driving onto the property often require directions to the registration area. Clear, readable and attractive signs provide that needed service. Vendors and suppliers, likewise, require direction to their authorised destination. If the hours which property can accommodate vendors and suppliers are restricted or limited, this information, too, will assist in the orderly conduct of business.

Speed must be controlled, and the normal method of such control is speed limit signs. Attention should be given to specific areas of greatest concern—pedestrian crossings, playground areas and areas of possible traffic obstruction or danger. Particular attention should be given to the lighting or reflective quality of speed limit signs. Additional vehicular-control limiting signs include signs which announce traffic direction limitation on turns and signs which announce destination limitations.

Designated parking, especially for employees, is a major access control consideration. Developing, using and enforcing employee parking has several advantages: it maximises available designated space for guest parking, it allows for better attention to employee personal protection, it reduces the likelihood of employee theft, and it allows for better control and safety of employee vehicles. Speeded bumps, when strategically placed, carefully and prominently announced, are often very effective in controlling speed in designated areas such as long, uninterrupted driveways or pedestrian crossings.

Devices designed to allow only one-way designated travel of vehicles are effective but should be used sparingly and carefully. Not only are the diagonally-positioned teeth a hazard in and of themselves, but inadvertent damage to tyres is not uncommon. Card access devices used most often for selected parking areas are less common in the lodging industry than in others. They are useful, however when circumstances dictate, but their expense should be considered.

The most common and useful technique of pedestrian access control is that of alarms and other electronic and mechanical deterrent devices. When such devices are used or considered, appropriate safeguards are essential. The maintenance department should assure appropriate factory mutual approval and proper code compliance. Perimeter and broad area protection devices, while common in many industry groups, are less so in the lodging industry.

Some applications exist, however, including the alarming of perimeter gates, usually installed with a central station annunciating capacity. Application is also not uncommon in protecting pool areas during off-hours. Point of entry devices are more commonly used in protecting window and door access points which cannot be otherwise monitored. Such devices are often hard wired to a central annunciation point and allow response when intrusion is attempted. In other circumstances, simple local alarm devices sound at the point of attempted intrusion. Several versions and approaches are possible depending on the circumstance—glass breakage devices; contact devices; heat sensor and movement devices are examples. The sophistication and capability of these devices increase consistent with their cost.

Restricting exit pedestrian traffic at designated doors is another example of access control and provides an effective and relatively inexpensive way of restricting access to designated doors which cannot otherwise be monitored. Some are simple local alarms which annunciate when unauthorised access is attempted, but this approach is often inappropriate because of the effect which such noise has on guests. Another softer approach, although more expensive, is hard wiring such alarms to a central annunciation point from which appropriate response can be dispatched. Obviously the decision regarding the type and placement of door alarms will be steeped in circumstances.

Surveillance cameras are not an uncommon approach to access control. They can be useful but their use and appropriateness depends on the circumstance for which they were designed. For instance, surveillance cameras are not usually an effective access control tool when immediate response is required. There are several reasons for this limitation in effectiveness. Not only must a constant and alert capability be maintained at the monitoring point, but also situation diagnosis is often difficult to accomplish. Additionally, response capability and time are often inadequate. Better uses of surveillance cameras are in those instances when a recording backup exists and can later be appropriately viewed and diagnosed.

Badges can be used for time and attendance purposes as well as for identification. If badges are issued on a daily basis, the system provides for a quick check on attendance levels. Different coded or coloured badges are useful for department and/or area access authorisation. Badges provide ease of access control when a discharge or termination situation takes place. Badges are available in a great variety of designs, materials and uses. Management is well advised to plan carefully prior to selecting a badging system. The issues for consideration include initial and replacement cost, the use for which the proposed system is anticipated, and the appearance of the badge itself.

In guest-room situations, particularly, employees should be encouraged and directed to encounter or report any person who has the appearance and mannerisms of being "out of the ordinary" or whose movements and body language suggest being lost, confused, or "suspicious". Obviously, if such a situation in any way suggests danger, the employee must be trained to call a predetermined person or department. When the employee is comfortable in a direct encounter, such should be encouraged. By reporting to predesignated persons or departments the appearance of persons who appear to be unauthorised, crime can often be deterred.

In the event that a person or group is encountered who turns out to be authorised, the mere fact of having encountered them tends to "put them on notice" and the likelihood of subsequent in appropriate behaviour is decreased. Every professional crime prevention authority agrees on the value of lighting as a deterrent. Studies performed in rural and urban centres, in industrial and residential districts, in virtually any and all settings, showed beyond a reasonable doubt that lighting is a deterrent to crime. This fact is no less true in the lodging industry.

Lighting decreases the likelihood of crime in parking lots, hallways and corridors, storage areas, and access points to buildings. Lighting is often extremely expensive. Not only can the uncontrolled use of lighting greatly affect the profitability of a property, but the initial installation can be a major undertaking and the maintenance required to insure continuing proper application also can be a burden. Another inherent problem with lighting often presents itself. Managers at the property level usually find themselves faced with a lighting situation over which they had little or no initial input. The property may have been several years or decades old when the managers began employment.

The initial style, type, placement, design, and intensity are conditions with which the manager must deal and over which they have little control. The dual challenges, therefore, of this countermeasure being both costly and difficult to manage sometimes cause the lodging manager to shy away from it as an effective crime-control measure. This propensity to overlook or ignore this very useful countermeasure should be avoided. While the manager may have limited ability to influence the placement, illuminating capabilities and style of lighting on the property, he does have the obligation to address the subject with whatever latitude he possesses. A written policy regarding lighting should be considered. This policy might describe required maintenance, including preventive maintenance.

Diagnostically, the existence and effectiveness of such lighting will be determined during the property survey. However, the effectiveness of the lighting and its proper balance in concert with other appropriate countermeasures such as access control will be developed during the examination and analysis by the protection management committee. Access points, both pedestrian and vehicular, at the perimeter and at the exterior of commonly used buildings should receive appropriate lighting attention. Crime deterrence is of particular concern in such settings.

Often less concentrated lighting is appropriate in broad open areas, but aesthetics and limited places where criminals could easily hide are considerations in these lighting decisions. Parking areas present classic challenges in so far as guest protection is concerned and lighting is normally required. Again, the decision on lighting should be made only after the diagnostic survey has been completed and the findings can be reviewed in conjunction with other appropriate countermeasures.

Normally the maintenance department conducts or directs the installation, maintenance and adjustment of lighting. Maintenance and adjustment should be accomplished on a scheduled basis and such maintenance should be documented. Work orders for lighting maintenance, like all guest protection-related work order requests, should be addressed in a timely manner. In many cases preventive maintenance has been found to be both operationally and economically effective. By replacing, for instance, entire banks or section of lights on a carefully timed and scheduled basis, labour cost savings may surpass the replacement cost of the lights even if they have not yet burned out.

Verification should be made that the work order has been received by maintenance and the work is being accomplished expeditiously. Employees in any and all departments who, in the course of their work, are in a position to view lighting, should be responsible for reporting instances of lighting malfunctions. This responsibility should obviously include instances of inoperative lighting but it should not end there. Instances of "troublesome" areas (e.g., pockets of darkness) should likewise be reported and the appropriate work order request submitted. Follow-up and verification should be accomplished.

The control of keys within the lodging industry is essential. For no reason other than the sheer volume of keys with which a hotel manager must deal, the problem of key control may be seen as overwhelming. In the face of this perception, however, two facts emerge which should mitigate temptations to ignore or mismanage key control. There are countless hoteliers active today who well remember the common use of the term "pass key". In today's lodging technological environment, such a word seems archaic, but even today, the use of such devices as key-in-knob locking systems and simple interior guest-room door hooks are not unheard of.

It is true that a vast number of smaller properties do not have the means to upgrade guest-room locking systems to a level many larger properties accept as a given. What must be stressed, however, is that regardless of the inherent level of effectiveness of a guest-room locking system, the requirement for key control within that system remains firm. The process of key control, while perhaps not perfectly circular, has no specific beginning and certainly no specific end. It involves a continuous series of actions, controls, requirements, and validations. It involves virtually every department on the property. And finally, it is multi-layered.

Locking and Keying Technology

The lodging industry is well aware that locking and keying technology has grown at a staggering pace over the past few decades. Such advance continues and it is a rare lodging magazine which does not advertise yet another newer and more advanced level of locking and key technology. Of further significance is the fact that virtually without exception the training in and maintenance of the key control aspect of such systems is a part of the offering. As such, the buyer receives not only a state-of-the-art system, but also instruction and training in its use. Those vast numbers of properties still relying on mechanical systems have no such advantage.

The emergency key is defined as "that key which can both unlock a double locked door and double lock an unlocked door". Consider that a guest, following advice given him on a guest-room posting, double locks his door by depressing the button located in the center of the inside guest-room doorknob. His belief is that he is virtually as secure within that double-locked room as a guest can become. What he may not realise, however, and what highlights the importance of protection for the emergency (E) key is the fact that anyone with that E key can bypass the double lock and enter that otherwise secure room.

There are several approaches to E key protection. Limiting the number of E keys is, in and of itself, a protective measure. There are properties which limit themselves to one and only one E key. The production of the E key should be under the highest of controlled circumstances. Production authorisation should be limited to a minimum of senior management personnel and such production stringently monitored and documented.

Issuance, like production, should be highly controlled and permitted only by the signature of the same limited number of senior management personnel. Unfortunately, possession of the E key often becomes a status symbol, being in the mind of the holder tangible proof of his elevated and important position and functions. Control and availability of the E key are both vital and inherent in its designed use. The E key must provide access to all locked guest-room doors. Additionally, some properties and indeed some political jurisdictions operate in modes whereby the E key also provides access to all emergency-related doors such as electrical and boiler rooms, elevator access, and fire-alarm panels.

While the E key must be maintained in the safest and most secure manner possible, it also must be available for obvious reasons at a moment's notice. Normally such availability is made to front desk personnel, on a controlled and recorded basis. The E key should be safely stored, ideally in a locked but accessible mode. When use is necessary, a record should be made of the date, time, circumstance of the use as well as the identity of all personnel having access during that emergency.

Some properties, even though they maintain an absolute minimum number off keys have found that a second E key securely maintained in the property safe and inventoried on a regular basis provides effective and sufficient back-up. Other than legitimate emergencies, no other use of the E key should be permitted. There is no known justification for an E key ever being permitted to leave a property. When the issue of guest protection and reasonable care is raised in a civil law suit, there is perhaps no more damning evidence suggesting the absence of such levels than that of' having given insufficient protection to this most vital tool. The master key is defined as "that key which can open all rooms which are not double locked".

A master key is designed to allow access to guest-room doors which have not been double locked, as well as to selected other locked rooms within a given area. There are levels of master keys, depending on the size and configuration of the property. Grand Masters are designed to open all doors on the property except double-locked guest-room doors. The use of these masters is becoming less and less common because of their vulnerability and the increased use of sub- or section- or building masters.

Sub-masters, as the name implies, are subordinate to grand master keys and are designed to access all doors, except guest-room double locked doors in a given area. Building masters, for instance, may access all such doors within a given building, floor masters may access such doors on a given floor, etc. Like the E key, strict controls and accountability are required for master keys. Whenever possible, masters should be subdivided into sub-masters. The loss or compromise of a sub-master is less serious or expensive to counteract than that of a master key. Assignment and accountability, too, support the division of masters into sub-masters. Sub-mastering and related appropriate issues and control procedures take into account this uneven access reality and allow for area as well as personnel departmental issuance.

Master keys should be accessible from limited sources. Often, they should be accessible, as is the E key, only from the front desk. On some properties masters have been permanently issued to key senior management personnel, such as the executive housekeeper. Even in these cases, however, the overnight or off-duty storage and control of the master is usually best assigned to the front desk. Irrespective of the location chosen for such a control point, the masters should be securely locked in a key cabinet or some other equally secure device and access/accountability carefully maintained.

Issuance of the master keys from the central control point should be in conformance with a system carefully designed and constantly monitored. Periodic review of persons authorised to issue as well as receive such keys is important. And issuance should be on a signature basis, limited to persons specifically identified by senior management. The key return likewise should be authenticated and inventory taken, ideally on a daily basis. The procedure should be in effect to immediately react when the inventory discloses a discrepancy. The documentation which verifies the issuance, return and inventory of master keys should be maintained and stored for an appropriate period of time.

Coding is often successfully employed by hotels in their master key control system. For example, by using a colour code tag system, one colour may indicate departmental sub-masters and another colour might indicate floor or building or section sub-masters. Such a tagging system aids in inventory control, issuance, and storage. The guest-room key is defined as "the key designed to open a specific guest-room which is not double locked". Like the E key and the master keys, centralised control of the guest-room keys is normally maintained at a central location, usually the front desk.

A key "par" should be established and the number of keys below par should trigger appropriate re-coring, re-keying, hardware rotation and/or production of replacement keys. The number of keys which constitute "par" is a matter of individual management decision but the adage that less is usually better is certainly apropos. Markings or fobs or engravings on the guest-room key should not identify the property. Room identification is best handled by eliminating the room identification from the key and supplying the key to the guest in a packet, card, or envelope on which is written the room number. Storage of the guest-room keys at the front desk should be in a secured drawer or cabinet, out of the view and access of everyone other than authorised personnel.

The front desk, housekeeping and maintenance are the three departments most involved in the key control process. The "beginning" of the circular route is the front desk. This department, generally speaking, is the focal point of the circular path which the guest-room keys will take throughout the property. Training of the front desk staff in the key control policies and procedures is essential if success is to be realised. This training should be a continuing process. Inventory of guest-room keys should be a matter of course and on a regular and scheduled basis, at least once daily. The ideal time for such inventory is often immediately after check-out time and appropriate inventory forms should be completed promptly.

Housekeeping, then should be placed into the inventory loop so that keys recovered by that department are considered. If re-keying, recording or rotation is appropriate, the affected guest-rooms absolutely should be placed out of service by management until this is accomplished. Guest-room keys are to be issued to registered guests only, normally at the time of registration. A method of recording the number of keys issued should be adopted and additional authorised issuance, should also be noted so that reconciliation can be made upon check-out. Both positive identification and authority must be obtained prior to issuing additional keys.

Additionally, guest-room numbers should never be audibly announced by the issuing front desk clerk. If the departing guest indicates his key or keys have been left at the guest-room, he should be assured that is perfectly acceptable and that housekeeping will retrieve the key during cleaning. On the other hand, often the guest has his key in his pocket and a simple courteous comment will serve as a reminder. When the front desk is alerted that a situation has occurred which might impact from a protection standpoint on the key control process, corrective action is called for immediately. Such procedures would be a part of the overall key control procedure and a continuing part of the training.

The housekeeping staff normally is the next department to become involved in the key control process. During the daily process of cleaning guest-rooms, room attendants will normally retrieve several keys which have been left, inadvertently or by design, by departing guests. Ideally a locked box securely attached to the housekeeping cart should be utilised to store these retrieved keys until delivery at the end of the shift. A responsible person should be assigned to transport all retrieved keys shortly after the end of the shift, back to the front desk so that they can be entered into the inventory.

Strict rules prohibiting the access of anyone to locked guest-room doors should be established and rigidly enforced. Room attendants should be instructed that requests from anyone to enter a locked guest-room door should be referred to the front desk or to senior management. Master keys should be secured on the room attendant's person at all times. Chains which allow both such security and required access are usually successful. The maintenance department could be labelled as that point on the "circular" key-control route where all things begin. While from the guest's standpoint the front desk is where the process begins, in actuality, it is in the maintenance department that the process has its roots. This is normally where the initial production occurs with the cutting of guest-room keys from the stored key blanks. This awesome responsibility, the ability to duplicate virtually any guest-room key at any moment, causes special attention to be focused on the maintenance department.

Key-cutting machinery should be well stored, controlled, and access limited. This machinery should be stored in a secure area, either in a room to which access can be rigidly controlled or if this is not feasible, then sub-compartmentalised in a secured cabinet. Access to the controlled room or the secure storage location should be by designated persons only. Key blanks should be controlled by a designated level of management—often the chief engineer or maintenance department manager.

Master and sub-master key reproduction requires special controls. Obviously a misplaced master or sub-master requires immediate attention, not only to replace the key but more importantly to re-key effected doors to which the misplaced master allowed access. Authority for such duplication and the adherence to quick and reliable re-keying should be vested in a predetermined level of management. Adherence to the required rapid re-keying in this situation is essential and should be audited on a frequent basis. When a bellperson escorts a guest to his room, he should be certain that the guest-room key is functioning properly and that the guest understands how the key operates.

Issuance of keys to the bell and valet staff should normally be controlled at the front desk. Van and courtesy drivers should remind departing guests of the necessity of returning keys and offer to accept from them any guest-room key which might have been forgotten. A locked box, not unlike that suggested for the room attendant's cart, is useful on vans and courtesy vehicles. All employees, irrespective of position or department, should be trained in the importance of key control. They should be aware of key control discrepancies and proper response.

Security is everyone's job. In fact, this slogan should be emphasised during an employee's initial orientation programme as well as in monthly departmental meetings. Successful prevention measures depend on a well-designed programme that involves input from all employees. The security manager can work with employees in a variety of ways.

First, he or she should educate employees about the seriousness of theft and how it affects them.

Second, she or he should attempt to develop employees' understanding of the problem in terms that they as members of the organisation can relate to and appreciate. For example, if it is made clear that all losses cut into the profitability of the property and that reduced profits, if severe enough, may result in lower wages or even laying off employees, the employees may realise that they too have a financial stake in the prevention of losses.

Third, assistance from employees may be elicited by encouraging them to call and report suspicious people or circumstances and at least make an extra effort to secure valuables when leaving a work area.

Fourth, it is essential that the security department maintain a good working relationship with all employees, avoiding morale problems created by poor communications and a lack of understanding. Employees suffering from poor morale are not going to be very concerned about protecting the assets of the employer.

Finally, the security manager must work with all other department managers to get their input on solutions to the problem of losses. Some security personnel may think that the solution to the loss problem is locking up and limiting access to the hotel's assets, but if a measure interferes with the normal operation of a hotel, it will be resisted and is a guaranteed failure.

8

Housekeeping and Sanitation

Housekeeping—shall pertain to cleanliness and orderliness of areas to include: washrooms, offices, passageways, aisles, storage areas, service floors, shops, laboratories and all other Laboratory facilities.

Practices and Procedures

Water

— Drinking water used by the Laboratory shall be tested routinely by the Plant Maintenance and Engineering Section to ensure uniform and proper consistency and compliance with all federal, state, or local sanitation requirements for both chemical and biological contaminants.

— The drinking water supply shall not contain impurities in concentrations which may be hazardous to the health of the consumer or which would cause offense to the sense of sight, taste or smell.

— The drinking water supply system shall be installed according to the National Plumbing Code and all other federal, state, and local plumbing requirements and shall be maintained in good condition.

— The drinking water system must be protected against backflow with connections and plumbing devices approved by the American National Standards Institute (ANSI).

— An adequate supply of potable water shall be available within a reasonable distance to any location at which employees are regularly engaged in work. Under certain conditions this requirement may be met by approved bottled water dispensers. These dispensers shall be designed, constructed, and serviced so that sanitary conditions are maintained and shall be capable of being closed.

— All water lines shall be distinctly marked according to the type of water flowing through them. Outlets for non-potable water, such as deionized water, distilled water, etc., shall be labeled to indicated that the water is not to be used for drinking, washing, or cooking purposes.

Food

— All foods and beverages shall be prepared, stored, displayed, dispensed, placed, or served in a way that they are protected from dust, flies, vermin, pollution by rodents, unnecessary handling, airborne droplet infection, overhead leakage, or other contamination to ensure compliance with all federal, state, and local requirements.

— Refrigerators located throughout PPPL must be labeled as to their contents with signs such as "FOOD ONLY" or "CHEMICALS ONLY." Refrigerators labeled for "FOOD ONLY" shall not be used to store non-food substances. Food shall not be consumed or stored where toxic or chemical materials are handled or stored.

— Microwaves used for food preparation are to be maintained in a sanitary condition at all times. Periodic inspection of microwave ovens is conducted by Safety Office personnel.
— All suspected or alleged cases of food poisoning must be reported to the Dispensary.

Waste

— All sanitary sewage shall be released from Laboratory controlled areas into sanitary sewer lines.
— Drainage through storm sewers and drainage ditches must conform with the water quality standards of the New Jersey Department of Environmental Protection.
— All chemicals and substances which are toxic, reactive, corrosive or flammable shall not be released into the sanitary or storm sewer system.
— All garbage and trash shall be accumulated outside of buildings in closed containers and shall be removed promptly from the premises.
— Items which are required to be recycled or are earmarked for scrap or special disposal shall be placed in designated containers.

Toilet and Locker Facilities

Adequate toilets, washrooms, lockers, and other essential sanitary facilities shall be readily accessible for employees near their work areas. These facilities shall be maintained in a clean and sanitary condition. Soap in a dispenser and hand drying apparatus shall be provided at each wash location.

Pest, Weed, and Animal Control

— A continuous programme of insect and rodent

abatement administered by Plant Maintenance and Enginnering shall be maintained.

— All pesticides, including those for use by contractors, shall be reviewed by the Safety Office for health and environmental impacts prior to use.

— Animal Control actions shall be initiated through Plant.

Maintenance and Engineering and shall be conducted humanely under appropriate local humane requirements.

— All herbicides or other chemicals used for grounds maintenance, including those for use by contractors, shall be reviewed by the Safety Office for health and environmental impacts prior to use.

All buildings shall be kept clean and orderly with:

1. Floors free of spilled liquids, debris,and clutter.
2. Light fixtures and windows clean.
3. Walls well-painted.
4. Machinery and equipment kept neat and in order. 5. Aisles clearly marked and kept free, with materials properly stacked in designated areas.

The floor of every workroom shall be maintained, so far as is practicable, in a dry condition. Where wet processes are used, drainage shall be maintained and false floors, platforms, mats, or other dry standing shall be provided where practicable, or appropriate waterproof and slip resistant foot gear shall be provided. To facilitate cleaning, every floor, working place, and passageway shall be kept free from protruding nails, splinters, loose boards, and unnecessary holes and openings.

An adequate supply of well-constructed, closed containers for trash, recycling materials, scrap, etc. shall be provided and emptied on a frequent basis.Aisles, doorways, and stairways shall be adequate for emergency escape, shall be plainly marked, and unblocked. Exits and emergency equipment, such as fire extinguishers, eyewashes, etc., shall be properly identified and readily accessible.

Procedures for periodic review to ensure the proper and prompt disposal of obsolete stock, parts, and waste shall be used. Excess chemicals, especially those for which a use is not foreseeable within the next six months, should be disposed of through the Hazardous Materials Section.

Sanitation and Health

In addition to facility, food, and water cleanliness, personal cleanliness is essential to maintain a healthful work environment. Inflammation of the skin (dermatitis) is an ever-present problem in an industrial or laboratory setting. Adequate washing and prevention of contact with agents harmful to the skin are the most effective measures of skin care.

- Wear clean clothing. Change clothing that has been contaminated with materials which may be harmful. Use disposable clothing as necessary.
- Use the proper personal protective equipment such as chemical gloves, face shields, aprons, etc.
- For minor exposures to relatively inert materials that cause excessive soiling, hand-protective creams may be applied before the job is started.
- Thoroughly wash after any job that causes excessive soiling of the skin and particularly after contact with agents harmful to the skin. Use hand-cleansing creams —not acetone, mineral spirits, and other such solvents —to remove greases, dyes, carbon, paints, resins, or other adhering materials. Hand cleansing creams do an excellent job and are available from stock.

— Solvent use can cause irritation of the skin. After excessive washing and contact with cleaning solutions and agents, handconditioning creams should be used to replace oil in the skin.

— Emergency showers and eyewashes are for emergency use to dilute and wash away contamiiiants in those critical seconds right after an accident in which you may be sprayed or splashed with a chemical. Employees should know the location of and how to use the emergency equipment nearest their work areas. Emergency showers and eyewashes are checked periodically by Plant Maintenance and Engineering. Emergency eyewashes should be flushed at a minimum of once per month.

9

Lodging Security

A wide spectrum of society is represented in the guest population; also represented are the problems the guests bring with them. Lodging industry professionals are clearly faced with a duty to act to protect guests. The security survey is an element in meeting the duty. Obviously, if the hotel staff is afraid to walk the sidewalk in front of the property after sunset, there is a real problem. While the hotel staff may be aware of crime in the immediate area and may in fact have developed personal strategies for dealing with it, the guests will have no awareness, no warning, and no personal defence mechanisms at hand.

Role fo Security Manager

A good way for the security manager to begin to appreciate the crime problem is to walk the area during various times of the day and week, and determine first-hand the types of activities occurring on the fringes of the property. A next step for the security manager is to establish working relationships with officers in local, county, and state law enforcement agencies. These may be the supervisors of patrol operations in the neighbourhood, vice squad officers, and robbery and burglary detectives. The security manager can learn from them the types and frequencies of crimes, the criminal methods of operation, and the nature of the criminal threats, e.g., whether the criminals act individually, in small teams, or as large gangs.

Printouts of crime statistics relating to the neighbourhood should be obtained and studied, along with the Federal Bureau of Investigation's (FBI's) Uniform Crime Report. The analysis of information collected through personal observation, interviews of knowledgeable law enforcement professionals, and crime statistics will help the security manager during the remainder of the survey to focus on vulnerabilities that may be exploited by the crime threat.

The security manager will follow a logical progression from analysis of threat to analysis of vulnerability to formulation of countermeasures. This is also another way of describing how the security manager will construct an overall protective programme. As a small example: in a walk-through of the neighbourhood the security manager observes gang activity (threat); joggers make up a good percentage of the clientele (vulnerability); the security manager asks for increased police patrol presence along the jogging route. In nearly all cases, this area will include parking areas. The swimming pool, tennis courts, and other outdoor recreational facilities might also be in this area. Other factors requiring consideration are: the perimeter, parking areas, exterior lighting, recreational areas, and the exterior walls of the lodging facility.

The security manager should examine the boundaries of the property to determine needs for psychological deterrents and physical barriers. It may be possible to inexpensively create boundaries by linking a natural barrier, such as a stream, with a hedge row, or by installing a short fence that extends from a fence or structure on neighbouring property. Lodging facilities are often constructed amid shrubbery and trees. Although aesthetically pleasing, these offer concealment to criminals who would prey on unsuspecting guests walking on the grounds or moving to and from their vehicles in the parking areas. Parking schemes for guests vary widely in the lodging industry. There is close-in parking, in which the motel guest's vehicle is parked within a few feet of the guest's room, garage parking, valet parking, on-street parking, parking lots in walking distance, and parking lots with shuttles to the facility.

Within the limitations imposed by the type and configuration of parking areas, the security manager must set up safeguards that primarily protect the guests and secondarily protect their vehicles. Good lighting is both a deterrent to crime and an aid in detecting and apprehending criminals. Lighting is a basic security tool that can also be pleasing to the eye; for example, when it is artfully integrated with foliage and water. Security lighting in a parking area is essential. Unfortunately, a parking area is sometimes not lit properly because management wants to avoid projecting an image that the lodging facility is in a high crime area.

In open general parking areas it is recommended that between 0.9 footcandles and 0.6 footcandles be maintained on the pavement. Lighting may go as low as 0.2 footcandles when there is a low level of night-time activity. In covered parking facilities, the recommended illumination levels increase to 5 footcandles for general parking and pedestrian areas; 10 footcandles for ramps and corners; and 50 footcandles at entrance areas. The security manager must consider the routes and means of transportation utilised by guests going to and from outlying recreational areas; the times of utilisation; the types of guests; and the valuables they may be carrying with them.

Security awareness should be second nature for all employees. It means being aware of the methods that criminals use, being able to spot suspicious persons and activities, and knowing what to do when the indicators are present. An awareness technique that incorporates both courtesy and attentiveness is for staff to greet persons who are on the premises and to offer assistance when it appears they are not sure of their bearings. To the guest, the employee making the greeting is seen as a helpful person; to a criminal looking for the opportunity to commit a crime, the employee is seen as a potential adversary and witness. Robberies at motels, motor lodges, and hotels occur more frequently than property owners care to admit. The foreseeability issue is strongly connected to robberies because of the potential for injury or death to guests and employees.

Employees should not be permitted to congregate in the lobby for two reasons. First, an unprofessional image is presented to arriving guests by the appearance of too many employees. The security manager will be concerned that a dishonest employee will have the opportunity to observe guests entering with expensive valuables and act upon this information or pass the information to a confederate. The guest-room is the traveller's home away from home; a sanctuary from the rest of the world. The major separating point between the sanctuary and outsiders is the guest-room door. The door should be a solid wood or steel door.

In most areas, local building codes and/or fire codes will specify doors with a specific fire rating. Hollow core doors should never be used at the entry point to a guest-room. The door should be equipped with at least one viewing port or peep hole. With the recent enactment of the Americans with Disabilities Act (ADA) serious consideration should be given to providing two peep holes in every door: one at a standard height and one at wheelchair level to accommodate guests in wheelchairs.

Whenever possible electronic locking systems should be employed that permit a "key/lock change" with every guest's arrival and departure. Electronic locks also make it possible to determine which key card was used to open a door at a particular time. This audit trail feature can aid investigations that involve unauthorised entries to guest rooms. It is not uncommon, however, to find smaller properties continuing to use the standard lock-in-knob arrangement, which is well known for problems associated with key control.

Professional thieves are always on the lookout for lodging employees who will sell or rent master keys. It is absolutely essential that mechanical locks be changed immediately whenever a key is missing. This includes keys that the guest forgets to turn in. The guest-room should not be sold to another guest until the locks have been changed. Each employee must turn in at the end of the work shift any lodging facility keys. It should be policy that only a responsible manager, such as the general manager, chief engineer, or manager of security, will be permitted to take keys off of the property. The door should be equipped with a deadbolt with at least a one-inch throw and self-closing hinges that cause the door to swing into a closed-and-locked position.

The self-closing feature must be reliable because guests will expect the doors to always and perfectly close behind them; if the feature fails, resulting in a loss or injury to the guest, the management can expect a claim for damages. The sliding glass or patio door often used in resort properties must be capable of resisting forced entry, including the technique of lifting a door panel out of its sliding track. The rule of thumb is to augment the locking capability of a sliding glass door with the use of a secondary device, such as a charley bar. Consideration must also be given to where a guest will store valuables.

Unlike office building security, where the office population is generally stable, the lodging security approach is tailored to address the unique problems of an unstable, ever-changing guest population. In coming to grips with these unique problems, the lodging security professional must take into account the diversity and the changing nature of the clientele. The relatively young lodging guests, those in their 30's and 40's, have different values and expectations than guests who are younger or older. The security manager must be able to balance the need for security, the guest's desire for privacy, and the organisation's need to reduce liability and losses. The structure, size, and reporting level of a security department will differ widely by hotel chain or company, due to the fact that there are presently no standards of organisational structure for certain size hotels.

However, these factors will affect a department's efficiency and success within a hotel. A typical department structure consists of the security manager, assistant manager, shift supervisors, and security officers. The structure ideally coincides with the size of the property, which usually is categorised by the number of rooms. In most hotels the department head usually will be called the director or manager.

A security department will encounter difficulties operating effectively with just a single person in charge. There will always be some situation to which the department head cannot attend, due to the usual limitations of a regular work schedule. A hotel cannot afford to depend on the availability of a single individual. The role of the assistant security manager should be just that—to assist the director/manager by shared job tasks such as scheduling, payroll, training, hiring and firing, and coordinating department meetings. The assistant in most hotels must be capable of working flexible hours and days. The management structure of a security department should include shift supervisors: individuals designated as being responsible for the officers working a given shift.

The supervisor is the vital link between employees and security management. The supervisor represents management's needs and views to the officers and at the same time has the responsibility of representing the needs and views of the officers to management. Without a knowledgeable supervisor available, the staff are left to make decisions in haphazard ways. A lack of structure could lead to an increase in poor decisions. Even if there are no actual supervisory personnel, some system of supervision must be in place. Little instruction material is available concerning the individual lodging security employee's role, contribution, or importance in the overall security function.

The size of a security staff required will generally be proportional not only to the number of rooms, but also to size of the facility and the number of employees on the hotel payroll. It also will depend on a number of factors that must all be considered simultaneously. In a pre-existing hotel, it is somewhat easier to determine staffing needs by reviewing the history of problems and guest-related issues addressed by security.

Other important factors to be considered include the design of the property and the location of the property relative to both the neighbourhood and the type of setting. An urban hotel in a high crime district should anticipate overflow problems from the neighbourhood, such as streetwalkers, vagrants, and trespassers. A hotel in a suburban location that is accessed only by motor vehicles and is surrounded by a residential community is less likely to experience the problems of the urban property.

Crime rates, economic growth or decline, climate conditions, and the availability of public safety resources such as police, fire, and ambulance services must all be taken into account when planning staff size and distribution. The level in an organisation to which security reports will greatly affect the ability of the department to achieve desired results. Lodging security departments have been known to report to a wide variety of managers, including the managing director, general manager, operations manager, human resources manager, building superintendent, and—perhaps most commonly—the rooms division manager.

A general manager's schedule is often so busy that it precludes regular accessibility except to a few senior managers. The security manager needs to be able to communicate routinely with the senior manager who oversees the security department. There are other problems caused by having security report to middle- or lower-level managers or to a manager who represents only one area of the company's operation. Each layer of management that security must penetrate to reach the general manager must be acutely and accurately aware of the problems. The more layers of people a manager has to communicate through, the greater the chances of misrepresentation. Not everyone in an organisation is an advocate for the security and prevention needs of the hotel.

It is clearly possible for a middle-level manager who oversees the security department to lack the enthusiasm needed to both advocate for and utilise security successfully. In order to maintain a global perspective, it is critical for the security manager to be aware individually of all aspects of the hotel's operation, including sales, accounting, human resources, and so forth. Some security professionals lack a broad company-wide perspective on the role of security.

Security solutions must be consistent with the overall operation of the hotel. The selection of security personnel must receive 100 per cent attention from the manager and/

or assistant. It is essential for all security personnel to be hired directly by the security department managers and not by the human resources department. In most cases hotels will hire personnel based on their immediate need, forcing themselves to hire the next available applicant. It has been a common practice for hotels to hire retired police officers and would-be police officers who for some reason have not been accepted onto the force and so work in security. There are clear pros and cons to this approach related to hiring managers, supervisors, or officers.

Many security managers are hired because they have a work history that includes experience such as law enforcement for a municipality or a federal agency. Traditional management thinking has been that this type of candidate has had extensive experience handling crime-related problems, is usually trained, and has many contacts within the police force or city/state government. For these three reasons, such a choice would seem reasonable and appropriate. Senior management must consider, however, the actual needs of their hotel. Not all properties are inundated with crime and seldom is the job of security solely focused on crime.

Furthermore, it is far more cost-effective to deter crime through broad-based prevention programmes than to expend resources trying to apprehend and prosecute criminals. Another drawback frequently encountered by hiring the retired local, state, or government employee is his or her view that the lodging security job is only a second source of income and, hence, not that important. These comments are not meant to say that no former police officers or government agents can succeed as security managers, because many have, but simply to point out the problems associated with their basic orientations, lack of management skills, and, perhaps, lack of incentive. A preferable candidate for such a position is one who is able to understand and work within a business organisation.

Hotels are more likely to have an emphasis on prevention, management principles, and labour issues, rather than on arrest and prosecution. Thus, a person with well-rounded management skills is far more likely to succeed than one who has a limited sense of the role of security. Security managers are the most important people in the security department because they set the tone of the organisation by their example. However, careful selection of other security personnel should be the second-most important task for security managers filling a department.

Lodging security is still a developing profession and, in some people's minds, is subordinate to police work. Many younger security officers see their positions as interim steps to becoming police officers. This is fine; working in hotel security allows them to develop experience and maturity. Although police officers currently may enjoy a better public image, they are not necessarily better paid, have better training, or have better opportunities for advancement compared to those in the lodging security industry. Still, many people do see lodging security as a path toward public law enforcement.

The problem human resources managers, or anyone else involved in the selection process, need to be sensitive to is hiring the frustrated would-be police officer who has been unsuccessful in getting a public sector job. It is one thing, for example, to hire a law enforcement or criminal justice student who wishes to gain experience. It is quite another thing to hire the individual who cannot be a police officer and must settle for the security job.

Promoting from within is a common practice for all types of organisations. The sense that you are getting someone as a supervisor or a manager who has established a track record and who knows the company is more comforting than hiring the unknown candidate. Prior performance, consistency, quality of work product, and reputation are all factors that should be considered. Positive and constructive discipline is training that corrects, moulds, or strengthens an employee in the interest of achieving departmental and hotel goals.

The effective disciplinary process condemns the act, not the employee. It is also important that discipline should be swift. Whatever the nature of the problem, be it simple tardiness or careless oversight, the long-range effect of coming to grips with problems immediately is better than putting off what probably will have to be faced later. The real essence and secret of constructive discipline is its preventive nature. To train, mould, and correct now reduces the need for more difficult training, moulding, and correction later.

Discipline is a responsibility that rests squarely on the supervisor's shoulders. It cannot be passed to a higher supervisor and should not be passed to human resources. Some weak supervisors shirk their responsibility with the idea that enforcing the regulations will hurt their relations with their subordinates. The supervisor who is fair and consistent in his or her treatment of employees will gain rather than lose respect through being firm and expecting conformity to the rules. Some make the mistake of believing that discipline is only directed at the inefficient worker. All employees require constructive discipline.

A hotel's reputation as a safe, well-run, clean, and comfortable establishment is essential for its success. The same argument can be made for the reputation of the security department and, certainly, the hotel's reputation will depend in good measure upon the success of the security programme. That programme's success is tied directly to the reputation and image of the department in the opinion of the hotel's employees, its guests, and the general public.

Capable and effective from the employees' perspective, the members of the security department and the manager, in particular, must project a positive image. Image is affected by a variety of factors, including outward appearance—grooming, demeanour and attire, personality (friendly and caring but professional at all times), consistency in treatment of employees in situations requiring security intervention, and emphasis on the positive aspect of services provided to fellow employees. It is a popular trend, for example, to eliminate the traditional security uniform and replace it with business attire. The security manager sets the tone for the organisation and should maintain positive interaction with all levels of employees, never using authority as a means of exerting influence or pressure on the employees.

From the guest's point of view, image and reputation will be determined primarily by the nature of the guest's contact, if any, with security while staying at the hotel. Most guests do not have any direct contact with security, and those who do will generally have it under adverse conditions, such as a theft of property or some other negative situation. Any victim, regardless of the seriousness of the loss or inconvenience, will behave in a fairly predictable manner, frequently blaming the security officer for not doing his or her job. It is essential that security personnel recognise that the guest's response is a normal reaction to stress. Furthermore, most victims know that it is unlikely that the harm they suffered cannot be undone and, therefore, really only look to the officer for some compassion and information.

Most victims simply want someone to listen to their plight, which suggests that the security officers must have developed good listening skills. To the outside world, the public at large, the reputation of a hotel's security department will depend on all the factors cited above, and the relationship the department and its members—

especially the manager—have established in the community. That community includes other hotels, the local police, the courts, the general public, visiting travellers, and criminals themselves, who have been known to have their own information system. Prostitutes, for example, know which hotels are easy to work in and which ones are not.

The security manager should make every effort to become involved in community activities related to crime and the hotel's business. Problems of crime will occasionally be so serious that police assistance will become necessary. A poor relationship with the local law enforcement authorities will impede solving such problems. Security personnel must be considered thorough and competent by the general public or the hotel security department will acquire a rent-a-cop image.

The most basic function for the security personnel in any hotel is to perform regular patrols of the property, both inside and outside. There are three different types of security patrolling that have been utilised in hotels for decades, yet continue to serve the needs of guests, employees, and the property in general: random routine patrol, lobby patrol, and basic rounds. In random routine patrol, the security officer walks, or in some cases drives, around the property on a random basis to check for irregularities, suspicious circumstances, and intruders.

Arsonists are known to use hotels as avenues for committing theft by setting fire to one location and, while everyone evacuates, stealing the guests' or hotel's property. Other arsonists like to watch people evacuate from buildings and will usually blend in with the crowd watching the scene. The typical arsonist has little concern for a facility's occupants or the firefighting personnel. Arsonists, particularly a professional "torch", will use flammable liquid in quantity.

Look for liquid containers that may hold accelerants that can turn a small fire into a major fire in a short time. One accelerant of which most people are unaware is the basic corrugated cardboard; it will burn intensely. Other items to be noted and acted upon include: dynamite charges connected with primer cord; hydrants or sprinkler valves that have been shut down or have deliberately damaged threads to prevent hose hook-ups; and unusual odours such as gasoline, kerosene, or fuel oil.

Documentation is essential to the proper operation of a security department in any environment. Reports usually generated by a hotel security department include incident reports, activity or shift reports, and safety rules violations. Well-written, typed, and accurate record keeping is very important and helpful to the future planning of the hotel in general and of security specifically. A security manager should be able to review the previous year or more of reports and identify patterns of activity that will help direct available resources in the security programme. Security reports are important as records for insurance or prosecution purposes; they should be thought of as important management tools, not locked away in a storage room or discarded.

Hotels offer a wide variety of services to guests, and like most other businesses they also maintain a lost-and-found department. The number of found items a hotel can accumulate varies with the size of the hotel and the volume of business within the hotel. Property that is turned in to security can potentially belong to a guest, patron, employee, or someone passing by the hotel. For ethical reasons as well as ensuring that all found property is secure, all lost-and- found items should be turned in to the security department daily. The property should be logged in and only given to its rightful owner on request.

Lost-and-found sheets are critical, as well as a lost-and-found log book tracking the property chronologically.

The company-wide manual covers policies and procedures that are general for the entire company. The manual may include vital, yet basic practices and procedures for each department within a hotel. This type of manual usually is used only as a guideline, while each individual facility develops its own manuals and handbook based on its geographic location. Most lodging facilities will also have a detailed manual for each department with emphasis on its operational departments. A separate manual specifically for the security department is an indispensable tool to give all security personnel the same information regarding the purpose, functions, and procedures carried out by the department.

Security department manuals typically contain a series of policies and procedures, directives, and references to information which may be critical to security personnel. Manuals should be designed for quick reference whenever a need arises and they also should be readily accessible. Little is accomplished when a well-written and well-designed security manual is locked up in the security manager's office after regular business hours. Ideally, every officer is given his or her own copy of the manual, and all manuals are updated as needed, generally on an annual basis.

Policies and Procedures for Security Operation

Policies and procedures need to be developed for every aspect of the security operation. By using a generic outline format, you can fill in the substantive information as you develop your manual. This ensures that there is a set way to deal with specific tasks and situations. Not all the employees of a hotel will have access to or even be aware of the existence of the security department's operation manual. Every hotel should, however, have a general company-wide policy and procedure manual that includes a variety of essential documents.

The fundamental policies and procedures of each department need to be covered in the company-wide manual. This is especially true in the area of security. Many people think security policies only involve how to patrol the premises or the methods employed when conducting an investigation. However, there are many areas that fall under the realm of security, and all hotel employees need to be aware of the appropriate steps to be taken in a multitude of situations that are likely to arise.

The hotel security department is an integral part of a business. Therefore, the security manager should think and act like a business manager. This includes generating various types of reports that disclose and describe the issues, problems, and concerns encountered by the security department. Many security managers spend too much time trying to support the efforts of law enforcement and lose sight of the fact that their departments are a vital component of the hotel.

The security manager must ensure that all essential parts of any incident report are written down by all security personnel and that they are the facts. Names, descriptions of individuals, vehicles, buildings, surroundings, correct dates, and times are critical when attempting to reconstruct on paper what actually took place. Often a report is not written immediately after an event occurs. Every security person should always carry a pen and a small pocket notebook to document key facts as they arise. Names, titles, and descriptions can often be noted quickly—even during an emergency. This information can prove to be critical months later.

The lodging security is changing daily. A hotel's reputation is, without doubt, its single most important asset. No matter how professional the hotel's services may be or how good a value may be offered, no one respectable will stay at a hotel if a bad type of activity is allowed to take place openly. It is probably safe to say that prostitution has been around as long as the concept of inns for travellers. Some of the comments frequently heard about prostitution is that it is a victimless crime and that society should not care what consenting adults do in privacy.

However, prostitution is a problem that, if not controlled, can ruin a hotel's reputation. The word controlled was used intentionally, for prostitution cannot and will not ever be eliminated. The security objective should be to reduce such activity to an absolute minimum. There are a number of simple control methods a hotel can employ. First, guest registration procedures must be established and followed closely. All guests must be required to show valid photo identification such as a driver's licence and preferably a credit card when checking in, even if they are paying cash in advance for their stay. The reason for the tight registration process is that most streetwalkers will not carry identification.

The housekeeping department will know if a certain guest-room has heavy traffic going to and from it and can alert security. There are two general types of problems associated with bars, restaurants, stores, and the front desk in a hotel. They are check and credit card fraud, and theft of merchandise including food and beverage items. Incidents involving "walk-outs" are common when non-paying customers enjoy a meal and/or drinks in a hotel and then proceed to leave without offering to pay for the items consumed.

Credit cards very often are used as a means of payment by patrons because of their convenience and the generation of tax records for business purposes. This convenience, however, has caused some problems for the hotel operator, particularly in food and beverage outlets and stores. The security department must face problems ranging from guests using stolen cards and cards over their allowable limit to dishonest employees inflating gratuities or even writing in gratuities. The best means of avoiding these and other scams is to develop detailed policies and procedures for authorisation of use, and to train employees to follow the procedures. Charging store merchandise to a guest-room, for example, must somehow be verified first.

Management must then follow up to ensure compliance with the rules, and violators should be dealt with appropriately. If security is called to investigate alleged wrongdoing by employees and the allegations are proven, swift and severe disciplinary action should be taken after all levels of disciplinary action are considered. Disciplinary action can range from counselling to termination.

The sale and use of illegal drugs are major issues in any industry, but appear more complicated in the lodging industry. The innkeeper must be concerned not only with employees, but also with guests and patrons who become involved with using and selling drugs. The use of drugs by employees on or off the job presents some serious consequences for both performance and safety.

With the cost of workers' compensation insurance rising so high and representing one of the largest line expenses for liability, employers must address the increased use of drugs by employees. Only recently have employers begun to consider the possibility that some employee accidents are directly related to drug use on or off the job. Morale problems are likely to arise among employees who want to do their job well, but see others not performing because of drug use. Furthermore, a work environment that allows employees to sell drugs to co-workers will create the impression that management does not care or is incompetent.

Security managers also can consider using undercover investigators posing as employees to determine who the dealer and buyers are, as evidence for termination. Drug use or sale by guests is not an unusual problem, but is one that hotel operators should be prepared to resolve. It is very unlikely that a hotel manager will be able to prevent a guest from using drugs in the privacy of his or her room. If however, the manager becomes aware of such use, action should be taken. Limited use (e.g., smoking a marijuana cigarette) may best be handled by warning the guest that repeated activity will result in removal from the hotel.

However, evidence of more serious use (such as large parties with cocaine left out in the open) may require assistance from the local police. It is common for drug dealers to use large urban hotels to conduct their drug deals, for the size of the hotel usually will ensure their anonymity. Certainly, no hotel operator wants to see her or his hotel aired on the evening news as a result of a major drug bust. Liaison with local, state, and federal law enforcement agencies is vitally important. Most law enforcement arrests involving drugs occur off property; however, the legal case may be developed around the actual activity that took place while on hotel property.

Training all hotel staff about drug activity awareness will assist security in preventing illegal sales, manufacture, or use of drugs on hotel premises. Depending on the size and location of a hotel, certain types of public figures are likely to stay as guests on occasion. In larger, convention-class hotels, political figures are often in attendance for social events. Public figures, whether they are politicians or people such as rock stars or sports teams, often will draw crowds. These crowds may be admirers, or they may be demonstrators protesting the appearance of the individual.

In either instance, security is faced with the difficult task of controlling the crowd while protecting the public figure. One should not assume that the local police will always take care of or even be aware of these problems. Instead, the security manager should be prepared to work with the authorities in planning for the person's arrival, stay, and departure. Occasionally, hotel security will not receive any advance notice of the person's arrival.

However, if your hotel security procedures include how to handle this type of scenario, coordinating this process should not take very long. Generally, though, there will be varying amounts of lead time available before the event. If this time is adequate, detailed planning will avert risk with minimal difficulty. The hotel may make reasonable regulations governing the conduct of its guests, provided such regulations are applied to all persons, without discrimination.

These regulations can be designed to prevent immorality, drunkenness, or any form of wilful misconduct, e.g., loud obnoxious behaviour, drug activity, etc., that may offend other guests, may bring the hotel into disrepute, or may be inconsistent with the generally recognised properties of life. The hotel has the right to evict any guest who wilfully violates these rules. Obviously, the eviction must be done in a reasonable manner. If guests refuse to leave the hotel after their attention has been called to the violation and they have been requested to leave and given a reasonable opportunity to do so, the hotel may forcibly evict them.

The hotel may use only such force as is reasonably necessary to accomplish this goal. Management personnel and security officers should be carefully instructed on this point and the hotel should obtain the assistance of the local police. When a hotel guest becomes ill with a contagious disease, the hotel management, after notifying the guest that she or he must leave, has the right to remove the guest in a careful manner and at an appropriate time to a hospital or other place of safety, provided this does not imperil the guest's life. As a practical matter, however, it is preferable to consult with an attorney and report these matters to the proper local authorities.

Usually the local authorities will take charge and remove the sick guest. The illness of an indigent guest should be reported to the local department of welfare, communicable diseases should be reported to the local health authorities, and psychiatric cases should be reported to the police. Security managers must ensure that they are knowledgeable about many types of crime, with special attention to those that may occur at a hotel—even if one would normally think they are unlikely to occur. For example, a hotel shuttle bus left a hotel an route to the airport with a group of tourists and was hijacked. The hijackers, posing as guests, had boarded the bus and waited. As it pulled out of the airport, one of the men pulled a gun and ordered the driver to head in another direction while his accomplice robbed the tourists of jewellery and money at gunpoint.

Floods, fires, hurricanes, blizzards, tornadoes, hazardous chemical spills, and power outages are some of the disasters that pose a threat to hotels. However, because it is nearly impossible to know for certain when these disasters will strike, hotels must have an emergency plan to protect themselves from these devastating events. Needless to say, this requires advance planning, and it can be challenging to imagine most risks. Once the risk analysis is completed, however, the security manager must determine priorities. Putting the risks in order of priority will also assist in creating a successful emergency plan. Within this plan, three separate groups of people need to be established.

The security manager should try to coordinate efforts from the "command centre" to cordon off and preserve damaged areas. The task of photographing, inspecting architectural designs for defects, and adding up actual damaged property claims and estimates needs to be accomplished as quickly as possible. Only after everything has been photographed and documented should the clean-up phase begin. Once a plan has been developed, it should be reviewed and critiqued by other management staff for accuracy.

The Hotel and Motel Fire Safety Act is designed to produce the safest lodging properties in the world. Most hotels have emergency plans and fire prevention equipment in place. However, more often than not, human error or failure is the root cause of life and property tragedies: Someone fails to report a hazard, or an employee disregards an emergency procedure even after he or she was trained properly. It should be noted here that any defence against fire must be viewed in two parts, fire prevention and fire protection.

Fire prevention, which usually is the hotel's major preoccupation, entails the control of heat sources and the elimination or isolation of the more obviously dangerous fuels. This commendable effort to prevent fire must not however, be undertaken at the expense of an equal effort for fire protection. Fire protection includes not only the equipment to control or extinguish fire, but also devices to protect the building, its contents, and particularly its occupants, in the event of fire. Fire doors, fire walls, smokeproof towers, fire safes, nonflammable rugs and furnishings, fire detector systems—all these are fire protection matters, and are essential to any fire safety programme.

A hotel should also have an outline within the procedures about how to handle the media. The community and others will want to know what exactly is going on. Designated media locations are important so that interference by the press is totally eliminated. Ad hoc interviewing of employees and victims of the crisis should be prevented. The media must not be allowed to manipulate a crisis scene into a three-ring circus. In most states, hotels are not required to provide medical services for their guests.

In busy hotels, however, a large percentage of the calls for security services will be medically related. These calls will range from simple abrasions and burns to serious trauma. Even if your hotel is in the middle of a large city with several hospitals and ambulance services, significant delays can be expected before expert assistance will arrive. Yet although many of the calls security receives in a given day will require some medical assistance, it generally will not be enough to justify the cost of a full-time physician who would need to be available twenty-four hours a day, seven days a week.

Security personnel, or any hotel employee who is likely to respond to calls for such services, must be properly trained. The key is to train for the level of services you are prepared to provide, and no more. Once medical assistance has commenced, you are expected to carry it out properly. The legal liabilities that arise against persons in such situations generally relate to how they performed the aid for which they were duly qualified.

Most hotels will have some level of emergency evacuation plans on hand. Whether the plans are simple or sophisticated depends on the security manager's exposure to disasters and knowledge of the subject. The risk analysis that the security manager conducts also will include evacuation vulnerabilities. Ensuring that a hotel can handle certain crowds is easy enough; however, ensuring that you can get the crowd out safely in the event of an emergency can be challenging. Evacuation from high-rise buildings is even more of a challenge. Usually there are only two avenues of travel up and down for high-rise buildings—elevators and stairs. The security manager must be aware that, in order to exit when an emergency occurs, human beings will naturally go toward the door through which they entered the hotel or function room.

Therefore, if a hotel uses ballroom exits only in case of emergency situations, someone has to be designated to inform the patrons and guests which way to exit. These guests and patrons also do not check for a hotel's fire exits when attending events such as weddings or dances. Another contributing factor to confusion in an emergency situation is when the room or corridor the crowd is in does not have windows, as this leads to a psychological effect which disorients people as to where they are and how to exit the hotel.

Hotel security departments must learn to overcome these types of problems until the time comes when elevators are made safe to use in case of an emergency. Evacuation plans for employees need to be established and detailed information must be provided so that step-by-step plans can be offered. New employees should get a basic overview of evacuation plans during their orientation programme within the first few days of employment. Additional training should be given once in a work environment or department. It is important for employees to be very comfortable within their environment, knowing the nearest exits and stairwells. Casinos are being developed in historic or refurbished structures, and river boats are being used to operate as floating casinos or moored casinos. There are also casinos in purpose-built facilities, which may have limited non-gaming amenities.

With gambling, there has been a trend toward allowing people to have greater control over their choice of activities and to be more responsible for the consequences of their own actions. But this principle has not been applied uniformly over the so-called "vices" such as alcohol, tobacco, illicit drug use, prostitution, and pornography. These vices have economic and social impacts on the hotel and/or casino similar to the impacts of gambling. The likelihood of these vices being introduced into the casino is very high.

Security managers should study their local gambling and lottery ordinances to find out what is and is not allowed. In addition, they should check with their local public prosecutor to find out what cases he or she is willing to act on and how the courts interpret gambling statutes. It is a known fact that the gamblers as well as persons who attempt to conduct scams are all well-versed in gambling laws. Don't be surprised to find people who attempt to challenge casino games, testing the parameters in order to commit acts which may be on the legal borderline. Likewise, don't be afraid to ask for help from a gaming investigator in identifying marginal cases.

The casino security strategy is people-watching, which is nothing new. Employee theft is not new, either, especially when millions of dollars pass through the hands of employees each day. As visitors and employees come up with new ways to cheat, many eyes should be watching. The most effective deterrent is people watching people, with most watchers out of sight. Hundreds of cameras can be hidden inside domes or behind ceiling panels. Pan/tilt capabilities, colour monitors, and strategic placement all contribute to cover every square foot of a casino floor. It is important for security staff to study what they see on those cameras to determine if angles should be changed, people should be followed, or if a zoom shot should be taken of a pile of chips. Most states allow tapes from casino crimes to be admissible as court evidence.

Crowding is a problem, due to the fact that river boat designers cram as many gaming positions onto each boat as possible, to take advantage of the enormous revenues generated from each position. One advantage to river boat owners is the fact that the boat is cruising—therefore, passengers do not have the option of leaving and frequently gamble more than they normally would. To alleviate the risks associated with congested spaces, security needs to be involved in the floor planning stage of construction to ensure that foot traffic patterns and passenger movement have been considered.

Another concern is that air circulation is poor in crowded spaces, and smoke-filled air can become an irritant, leading to a less-than-optimal gaming experience for many guests. Surveillance is very important in casino security environments, where criminals range from casino dealers and employees to "railbirds" who steal chips from the sides of tables while patrons are not paying attention.

Surveillance specialists look for targets of theft where the stakes are high. Crimes take place in areas of intense action, where more chips are being played or the value of the game is high. Surveillance specialists also look out for known troublemakers and have a central supervisor or pit boss for every ten tables.

Usually, the staff working in surveillance security have worked in hotel security and are knowledgeable enough about guests' traits and mannerisms to assist them in identifying problem people. Another issue for casino security is that the budget needs are far greater than most security departments' needs, due to the vast amount of technology necessary to conduct professional surveillance operations.

Storage of video equipment, for example, is an important factor because tapes must be retained in case they are needed for prosecution of criminals or other legal matters. Most surveillance specialists are concerned about having updated and timely identification of known criminals, along with their method of operation.

Casino security and hotel security, as professions, need to be recognised as excellent career paths that offer upward movement. These positions develop special talents that should be rewarded accordingly. Both education and experience must be continuous and security professionals must be allowed to grow with the industry. Hotel chains that have surveillance experts need to allow them to assist the industry as it grows by sharing information, training, knowledge, because it is not a competitive area.

Every security department—regardless of the lodging facility size, number of employees, or even number of security staff, for that matter—must have some form of training. Training programmes for security employees fall into two separate categories: a programme for newly hired staff, and regularly scheduled training or ongoing training for staff. From a potential liability perspective, it is essential to train all security employees before they handle calls on their own and, further, to ensure that the training programme reflects the actual job.

Inadequate training has been a major downfall of lodging security for years. This is also an area that receives the most criticism whenever legal issues arise about an incident. Inadequate training claims are based upon either spending an insufficient amount of time on a topic and/ or not addressing issues that will be encountered on the job.

For example, if a security officer routinely receives calls for medical assistance, it would be unreasonable not to provide some training in basic first aid. The need for improved training is higher now than ever because the pressure from the public (guests and patrons) has been compounded with the recent recognition of crime rates.

Most people today in any profession are measured by the amount of education and training they have received, which qualifies them to perform their job. For lodging security professionals, both proficiency and success are based on experience and training. Keeping abreast of the current lodging security issues is another important factor. All lodging security personnel should receive the same initial orientation and policy handbook as every other employee. Then, when the security staff members arrive in their departments, the training programme is outlined in respect to their positions.

Management often was reluctant to involve security because it had questionable confidence in the staff. Instead, it handled liability issues in a public relations fashion. With the phenomenal growth of litigation throughout society, and particularly in the lodging industry, security has taken on major responsibility to investigate, report, and develop prevention programmes for many of these problems. Hence, it makes considerable sense, for example, for the contemporary hotel security manager to be responsible for overseeing and managing most general liability problems, including the loss of guest property, claims of guest injury, damage to or loss of guest vehicles, and employee accidents.

The most common claim guests make against a hotel is that some of their property has been stolen from their guest room. Security personnel must be cautioned not to assume that all reports of lost property necessarily mean that the property has been stolen. It may simply be misplaced or missing. It is common for victims of loss to blame someone else.

Therefore, adequate information must be gathered to determine whether the item was in fact stolen or simply misplaced by the guest. The reason is obvious—lost property requires one type of investigative approach, while stolen property involves another. In a lodging setting, however, the guest, unless he is informed, cannot be expected to understand and appreciate the threats that exist which are peculiar to that city, that neighbourhood or to that property.

There are, however, some protection considerations which are virtually universal and which should be incorporated into any guest-room protection countermeasures. Confidentiality of the guest-room location is vital. No audible announcement of the guest's room number should be made at the front desk or at any location.

When providing the key to the guest, he should be informed of the room number by the use of a card or key holder or some other nonverbal means. Obviously, when the bell staff is used, the room number again should never be verbalised but rather the bellperson should be informed of the room location in the same confidential manner by which the guest was notified.

When receiving inquiries regarding a guest, whether by phone or in person, the confidentiality must again be maintained. A guest's right to privacy is a vital and long-standing tenant of lodging and should never be violated. When a request is made for a room key by a person claiming to be an occupant of that room, positive identification must be made of that person prior to issuing a key. Standard identification methods should be established and used as appropriate.

The locking system utilised at the guest-room door is a major consideration in this countermeasure. Basically systems available to the hotelier fall into one of four general categories. They are key in knob, standard mortise locks, mortise locks with programmable cylinders and/or removable cores, and electronic lock systems.

Key-in-knob is a system in which the key channel is actually within and a part of the doorknob itself. It is activated by inserting the key directly into the knob and the channel. This is probably the least effective of all systems, is considered generally insecure and in fact is prohibited in some states as a hotel/motel guest-room locking system. The word "mortise" means, literally, "a hole, groove or slot into or through which some other part of an arrangement of parts fits or passes".

This system usually consists of a face plate, with the doorknob and an unconnected separate key channel on the exterior side of the door and a deadbolt arrangement on the interior side of the door. Mortise locks with programmable cylinders and/or removable cores allow for quick key combination changes. Electronic lock systems allow for a unique selection of keying combinations whenever a new guest is assigned to that room, whenever a compromise or key loss is suspected and whenever management determines that such action is warranted.

New and more sophisticated systems are reaching the market on a continuing basis and the choice for the hotelier is a difficult one. If there is a single rule-of-thumb to follow, it is that whatever system is chosen, it offers higher protection if the locking combination can be changed on a random or programmed basis whenever required. Door and frame construction as well as attendant locking hardware should be of such quality and workmanship as to minimise the ease by which an intruder can bypass them by force. Obviously, the hinges should be located to preclude the pins being pulled from the exterior.

Self-closing automatic locking devices should be standard. Connecting room doors are those doors which are placed between guest-rooms to allow for access from one guest-room to another or to enlarge the rented space from one-room to two-or-more-room capacity. Historically, these doors often have been of lesser construction than the main guest-room door.

In fact, the threat which is posed to the guest by inappropriate connecting room door design, maintenance or construction warrants special attention. Single connection door arrangements are strongly discouraged. Instead, there should be two separate doors, each void of all hardware on the inside.

In effect, then, there are two doors facing one another, neither with locking hardware and with space between them. On the guest-room side of each door, however, there should be provision for the guest himself to provide added self-protection. Only guests occupying both rooms simultaneously and in concert with one another or hotel/motel staff should have the ability to access both rooms.

Many door locking systems have a double locking dead bolt and single action panic release features installed within the system. Many states require the hotelier laws of that state to be posted prominently within the guest-room. The limits of liability in so far as the loss of personal belongings are normally shown and are posted so that the guest understands those limits.

Also, normally noted on these postings are the considerations of safe deposit and property safekeeping facilities available at the property. All too often, however it is the hotelier himself who has not kept his knowledge current. Announcements concerning what actions the guest ought to take in order to secure that door to the fullest extent possible should be posted on or near the back of the guest-room door.

All double locking procedures should likewise be explained. Use of the view port and methods of securing any connecting or sliding/patio doors should also be addressed. Personal injuries due to accidents occur more often in the bathroom than any other portion of the guest-room. Postings, therefore, regarding tub safety, use of any grab bars, slip-and-fall deterrent bathmats, etc. should be considered. If particular use of electrical equipment in the bathroom is desired, warnings regarding their use should be posted.

The guest-room telephone is more than a convenience. It can be, literally, a life-saving guest protection device. Several methods are possible to accomplish this immediate handling of any emergency call. The emergency number can be channelled, like all operator calls, into a central switchboard. If this is the system chosen, care should be taken that when the emergency number is dialled, it has an extremely distinct ring—much louder perhaps or with a distinct tone.

The use of a warning light which is activated along with the distinct ring adds greater assurance that the operator will note the call immediately and cease all other duties to respond to it. The emergency line might also be channelled into a continually manned security office, dispatch point or control centre. Again, the ringing apparatus and arrangement must be such that the ringing tone is clear, distinct and unique and is inevitably responded to immediately.

Automatic taping of the ensuing conversation is a plus.The lodging industry is long past the time when it was felt that education of guests about threats and dangers and protection methods were contrary to the "host image". On the contrary, such announcements and notifications are now considered absolutely essential by most professional hoteliers.

The bell staff should be scripted and instructed in all protection aspects of the guest-room. They should direct the guests to the TV announcement, if there is one, even turning the TV on and to the particular announcing channel so that the guest gets an early opportunity to view and hear it. The bellperson should also call to the guest's attention the guest-room service directory and highlight the fact that there is a section regarding protection. Finally, the bellperson should mention the entire range of protection devices, techniques and announcements present in the room.

10

Maintenance of Culinary Service

In every hotels, all refrigeration units must have numerically scaled indicating thermometers accurate to $\pm 3^\circ$ F with the temperature-sensing unit located in the unit to measure air temperature in the warmest part. All such thermometers should have an externally mounted indicator to facilitate easy reading of the temperature of the unit.

Adequate facilities must be provided to promote good hygienic practices, sanitary food handling and to minimise the potential of cross contamination between finished and raw products. Separate areas should be designed to separate food handling operations involving raw and finished products. Separate vegetable washing facilities shall be provided in establishments that wash raw vegetables. Where it can be documented by low volume, infrequent preparation or where items are purchased prewashed and pre-packaged, a separate preparation sink may not be required.

Establishments that scale or eviscerate fish, wash raw poultry, or other raw meats shall provide separate sinks with preparation space for these processes. Where it can be documented by low volume, infrequent preparation or where items are purchased prewashed and packaged a separate preparation sink may not be required. For facilities that have a low volume of vegetables, fish, poultry or other raw meats that are being prepped or washed then the operator may want to install a chief table to accommodate this operation. The minimum recommended drainboard length for food preparation sinks when installed is 18".

Approved food containers with tight-fitting covers are required for storing broken lots of items such as flour, cornmeal, sugar, dried beans, rice and similar foods. Scoops are recommended for each food storage container in use. Facilities that have a large amount of take-out or use single items will need to increase the amount of storage in order to handle these items.

Lavatory facilities shall include hot and cold running water supplied through a combination faucet or tempered water, sanitary towels or approved hand drying devices, and soap. Antibacterial soap should be provided at each employee lavatory facility. Any self-closing or metering faucet should be designed to provide a flow of water for at least 15 seconds without the need to reactivate the faucet. For employees, at least one lavatory facility shall be provided in the kitchen area in addition to any lavatories which may be provided in the toilet rooms.

Additional lavatories may be required in food preparation or utensil washing area which are more than 25′ from a lavatory or when the food preparation areas or utensil washing facilities are located in a separate room. Splashguard protection is required if spacing to adjoining food, food contact surfaces, or utensil washing and storage area surfaces are less than 18 inches. Splash guards shall not hinder access to the lavatory, should extend from the front of the sink to 12 inches above the rim of the sink, and be of easily cleanable construction.

Sewage Disposal System

Cross-connections with sewage lines; unapproved water supplies or other potential sources of contamination are prohibited. Hot and cold running water under pressure shall be provided to food preparation, utensil and handwashing areas, and any other areas in which water is required for cleaning. Running water under pressure shall be provided in sufficient quantity to carry out all food preparation, utensil washing, hand washing, cleaning, and other water-using operations. The following outlines some of the equipment installation requirements to insure proper spacing and sealing to allow for adequate and easy cleaning.

Installation of Equipments

Drainboards may be manufactured with continuous side and back splashes and mounted directly to the adjoining wall area. Backsplashes must adjoin the wall within 1/32 of an inch and be caulked and sealed to create a smooth, sanitary, vermin proof installation. Where equipment does not effectively adjoin the wall within 1/32 of an inch it should be installed a minimum of 3 inches off the wall. Soiled Drainboards are recommended to be located a minimum of 18" from food contact surfaces or equipped with splash protection. Splashguard protection is required if spacing to adjoining food, food contact surfaces, or utensil washing and storage area surfaces are less than 18 inches. Splashguards shall not hinder access to the lavatory, should extend from the front of the sink to 12 inches above the rim of the sink, and be of easily cleanable construction.

Food equipment that is small and light enough to be easily moved by one person shall be considered portable and is exempt from equipment installation requirements. Undercounter equipment installed on the floor shall be equipped with casters or sanitary skids, or on 6-inch sanitary legs and sealed to adjacent surfaces or properly spaced to facilitate cleaning.Casters shall be properly sized for the equipment served, and should be compatible with the cleaning materials used. It is strongly recommended that equipment be installed on casters when possible. Equipment installed on casters allows easy movement and facilitates the cleaning of surrounding surfaces and equipment. Casters also allow for maximum utilisation of space by reducing or eliminating spacing requirements for cleaning.

Island installation of equipment reduces the total floor area that must be cleaned. Masonry islands should be a minimum height of six inches with a cove of at least ¼" inch radius at the juncture of the island and the floor. The edges of the equipment should overhang the island (but not more than the height of the island) to prevent grease or other liquids which may spill over or run down the sides from running underneath. The juncture between the base of the equipment and the island shall be sealed to prevent vermin harborage. Equipment not readily movable or sealed to adjacent surfaces shall be spaced to allow access for cleaning. The amount of space required between and behind equipment depends on the size of the equipment and the accessibility needed for cleaning the equipment and adjacent surfaces.

Equipment placed directly on the floor, such as counters, display cases, cabinets, proofers, ovens, large cooking kettles and retarders shall be effectively sealed to the floor using silicone, metal flashing, vinyl coved base, or other approved material. Metal kick plates which are readily removable will not be required to be sealed to the floor, provided the base of the equipment is sealed to the floor or the areas behind the kick plates are easily cleanable.

Equipment attached to walls, such as lavatories, preparation sinks, utensil washing sinks, dish tables, counters, and cabinets shall be effectively sealed to the wall to prevent splash, debris accumulation, and vermin harborage. If the equipment is open underneath, such as a drainboard, dish table, or open base table, it may be installed at least three inches away from the wall.

Dishwashing Facilities

Hand dishwashing facilities should include an approved three-compartment sink. The sink shall be of sufficient size and depth to submerge, wash, rinse and sanitise all utensils. The sinks shall have splashback protection and drainboards that are an integral part and continuous with the sink. Adequate facilities shall be provided to air-dry utensils. This may be accomplished by approved drainboards, dishtables, portable or stationary air drying racks, or wall and/or overhead shelving units located in close proximity to the dishwashing area. Floor drains should be provided in areas where wet pots, utensils and equipment are air-drying on approved racks or dish tables away from the sink.

Dishwashing facilities are recommended to be located such that dirty dishes from the dining area are not carried through food preparation, storage or display area. Dishwashing equipment should be located immediately inside the kitchen door when entering from the dining area. This location will reduce the possibility of contamination that can occur when dirty dishes are transported through the kitchen and food preparation areas. Adequate facilities shall be provided to air-dry utensils prior to final storage. This may be accomplished by approved drainboards, dishtables, portable or stationary air drying racks, or wall and/or overhead shelving units located in close proximity to the dishwashing area. Floor drains should be provided in areas where wet pots, utensils and equipment are air-drying on approved racks or dish tables away from the sink. For air drying of utensils it not necessary to have large drainboards.

Backflow

Backflow is a reverse flow in the primary or secondary system that is opposite to the expected or intended direction. This flow reversal is undesirable; however, a properly protected system can remain safe. There are two types of backflow, acting separately or in combination, that allow contaminates (high hazard) or pollutants (low hazard) to enter the water supply via a cross connection: backpressure and back-siphonage. Backpressure occurs when both systems (potable & nonpotable) are under pressure, but the nonpotable system has a greater pressure than the potable system. This pressure differential pushes the contaminant or pollutant into the potable supply.

There are several different types of assemblies (units that can be tested after installation) and devices (can not be tested after installation) available for controlling cross-connections and preventing backflow. Low Hazard situations exist when there is an actual or potential connection for a nontoxic substance (also referred to as a pollutant) to be introduced to the water supply and create a nuisance, or be aesthetically objectionable to the water user. Examples of pollutants are turbidity, beverages, and food coloring.

It is simple, economical, non-mechanical (no moving parts), fail safe, and can be used for potential backsiphonage or backpressure situations. An air gap is an unobstructed, vertical air space that separates a potable system from a nonpotable system. This air gap is necessary to prevent any contaminant or pollutant from being siphoned or pushed back into the potable water supply.

Although this is an extremely effective backflow preventer, the interruption in the piping creates a subsequent pressure drop on the "down stream" portion. Consequently, most air gaps are used at the end of the supply line or faucet such as at a sink, vat or storage tank.

Mechanical Assembly or Devices

The type of mechanical assembly or device selected must be appropriate for the degree of hazard and specific application relevant to the potential backflow possibilities. Mechanical backflow preventers consist of single or multiple check valves that open from the flow pressure of the potable water. These valves are fabricated to seat tightly on a machined surface and when closed, prevent any flow in the wrong direction. Also, some devices have air inlets or ports that are vented to the atmosphere to relieve any vacuum or negative pressure developed in the system. All backflow devices must be installed so they are accessible for inspection, service and repair.

Oil and grease entering a facility's drainage waste system will eventually solidify somewhere'- down stream and eventually clog the sewer line and/or cause potential problems for the onsite or public sewage system. The oil and grease from foods and cooking liquefy at high water temperatures primarily originating from the three compartment sink, warewashing machine or some pieces of equipment such as an oriental wok cooker.

Trap installations are designed and sized based on anticipated flow rates and organic load for maximum efficiency. Specific gravity (density) of the grease filtrates affects the time necessary for separation. For example, the specific gravity of water is 1.0, thus the lower the specific gravity of the oil, the less time it takes to separate and float to the top of the tank. Also, the higher the flow rate, ratio of grease to water, suspended solids, and total grease volume to be retained between cleaning/emptying, the larger the grease interceptor must be. Grease traps range in size from 35 gallon units located inside the kitchen area to 1,000 gallon inground installations outside the facility.

Screening for windows, doors, skylights, transoms, intake air ducts and other openings to the outside shall be tight fitting and free of breaks in the screening material. Screening material should not be less than sixteen mesh to the inch. Doors, door jams and openings between the floor and bottom of outer doors shall be adequately flashed with a rodent proof material to eliminate any openings. Openings within the establishment around pipes, or conduit shall be tightly sealed.

Openings on the outside of buildings shall be sealed with sheet metal, concrete or brick and mortar. Eliminate potential vermin harborage by sealing all cracks and crevices. Cracks and crevices in excess of 1/32" shall be sealed with an approved caulking compound to provide a smooth and sanitary installation. Horizontal spaces, which will be rendered inaccessible after construction or equipment installation (such as wall cavities and areas underneath walk-in coolers or cabinets), should be treated with an approved material to prevent the possibility of roach infestation. Loading docks and delivery doors should be provided with effective air curtains, vestibules, or with self-closing doors to preclude the entrance of insects.

VENTILATION

Ventilation systems shall be designed and installed according to state building codes. There are several methods used in calculating the volume of air movement, measured in Cubic Feet per Minute (CFM), necessary to effectively and efficiently ventilate cooking equipment. While these methods are used in general applications, it must be noted that engineered exhaust systems which are customised for specific equipment under specific use conditions may also be approved by the building code official or fire marshall.

Exhaust: The purpose of an exhaust hood is to provide a method of collecting, as nearly as possible, all of the grease produced from the cooking process, while furnishing a means of removing heat, smoke, and odors from the cooking area. For the hood to fulfill its purpose there must be a sufficient volume of air movement (capture velocity) to draw grease particles and cooking vapors directly from the cooking surface to the grease extractors. This air flow removes cooking odors and keeps grease particles from settling onto nearby surfaces. An effective capture velocity shall be sufficient to overcome opposing air currents, capture the grease and cooking vapors, and transport them directly to the grease extractors.

Grease extractors are ineffective in removing grease vapors. Only when grease vapors cool and condense can an extractor remove grease particles by directed air flow, contraction, and expansion (drop out). It is essential to have a sufficient volume of air flowing to cool and condense the grease vapors into grease particles prior to reaching the grease extractors. Non-toxic smoke bombs may be used to evaluate and regulate kitchen exhaust hoods and supply systems. No fabricator of exhaust hoods can create all the conditions in the plant that the hood must cope with on the job site to function correctly. In the case of heat and steam producing equipment, the purpose of the hood or ventilation system (such as a pants-leg duct system) is to control humidity, heat, and unwanted condensation.

Ventilator hoods shall extend from the wall a minimum of 16 inches, and shall be installed so that the distance from the top of the cooking equipment to the bottom of the ventilator hood is no more than 24 inches.

Equipment placed under a ventilator hood shall not extend beyond the sides of the hood or more than 36 inches from the back of the hood. These restrictions are necessary to ensure maximum capture and removal of cooking emissions.

The amount of air exhausted through a hood exhaust system is dependent upon the size of the hood, its particular installation, and its use. Exhaust ducts should never be located at the sides of the hood. For hoods that are six feet or less in length, only one outlet should be provided. Long hoods should be provided with multiple outlets no closer than six feet apart and no further than 12 feet apart. For hoods equipped with multiple ducts, it is advisable to install a manual air volume damper on each outlet so that the system can be easily balanced.

Extractors have generally replaced wire mesh filters where grease removal is of prime concern and compliance with National Fire Protection Association (NFPA) codes is required. Wire mesh filters may be used to exhaust pizza ovens, bread and pastry ovens, and other similar equipment where grease is not of prime concern. Both wire mesh and extractor type filters have an efficient operating velocity range of 200 to 500 fpm; the operating velocity of the filters shall not be less than 200 fpm.

There are two general types of grease filters: wire mesh and extractor filters. The extractor filter removes grease in the exhaust process by centrifugal motion or by impingement on a series of baffles. The manufacturer's optimum rating of the filter should be used in calculating the filter area required in the exhaust system. Standard size filters should be used to avoid additional cost and to allow ease of replacement. Any space in the filter bank not covered by filters/extractors shall be fitted with sheet metal blanks.

Recycle Containers and Facilities

Cleaning facilities shall include a combination faucet, hot and cold or tempered water, threaded nozzle, and curbed impervious pad sloped to drain or other approved methods at the facility. Where containerized systems (compactors) are used for garbage storage, facilities shall be provided for the cleaning of such systems. Cardboard storage containers shall be stored on concrete pads or other impervious surfaces so as to prevent rodent harborage. Dumpsters shall have drainage holes plugged when not being cleaned.

Water should be accessible to cleaning area and not over 50 feet away. Surface water restricting valves shall be used where Municipal Sewage Departments or on site sewage disposal system requires restriction of surface water. The problem that has come up in many municipalities is that some will not allow for these drains to be installed for fear of rain water coming off the pad will overload the municipal sewage treatment system. This can be avoided be installing a sump in the pad which has a double outlet.

When the cleaning operation is finished the switch is turned off and any rainwater that enters the sump will drain directly out into the storm drain. By installing this type of system two concerns are addressed; one being that the waste is now properly disposed of, and the other is satisfying the concern of excessive rain water impacting the municipal sewage treatment system.

FOOD SAFETY

According to Travel Industry Association of America (TIA), in the wake of 9/11, business travel fell 9 percent while leisure travel was actually up 2 percent, but more leisure travelers arrived by car — attributable both to budget constraints and fear of flying. Those wishing to expand during the coming decade can no longer target the upscale, businessperson for whom dining out is less of a novelty, spends more and may be more focused on high quality, consistency and convenience.

The leisure traveler, especially those who are less frequent restaurant patrons, crave a unique experience along with a friendly more approachable environment.To achieve individuality visit all the competition in your category and take detailed notes. A word of caution, while it is tempting to go upscale during a renovation, many successful restaurants risk pricing themselves out of the market or losing segments of their customer base, such as the lunch crowd. While creativity and innovation are hallmarks of a truly outstanding culinary experience, it is a daily focus on the basics that makes a foodservice operation profitable.

Every recipe for every menu item, both à la carte and catered, must be standardised and costed. This basic discipline ensures consistency of product and ongoing profitability. While the initial set up requires some effort on the part of the chef, it allows each item to be priced based upon its raw ingredient cost. Given the volatility of some ingredients, it is important to revisit recipe costing on a periodic basis. One way to simplify this process is to set up each recipe on a separate worksheet in an MS Excel® file. By linking each recipe ingredient to a master ingredient list, the chef can easily update the master list, hence all recipe costing, on a monthly basis.

The standard method of pricing is to take the cost of each menu item and multiply it by an appropriate multiplier to cover the cost of labor, other expenses, and overhead. For instance a 2 ½ times multiplier should yield a 40% food cost; a 3 times multiplier yields a 33% food cost. This simple formula is all well and good, but if your revenues are below projections and/or your payroll cost or overhead are higher than expected, you may still lose money.

Standardised recipes are costed based upon specific portion sizes. If untrained or poorly supervised employees routinely serve larger than costed portions, you can kiss your profitability goodbye. Costly meat and fish products should be weighed to ensure correct portion size. Ladles of specific sizes should be used to plate specific menu items. Pies, cakes, and other baked desserts should be cut and served using templates to ensure the correct number of portions are realised. Cooks and pantry workers must be trained to prepare and serve appropriate sized portions.

Electronic timekeeping systems make it easier for supervisors to verify employee hours, but regardless of system used, supervisors must monitor payroll hours daily. Close monitoring of employee hours will reduce overtime and milking the clock, while allowing daily comparison of payroll cost to revenues. Front- and back-of-house supervisors should also keep a daily log that notes revenues, meals served, payroll hours, and a subjective evaluation of the smoothness of service. Benchmarking is the act of measuring and analysing operating performance.

In a food service operation there are many things to benchmark, such as meals served and average check per meal period by day of week; payroll hours by position by meal period or day; and beer, wine, liquor sold per meal period and day of week. When tracked over time, these statistics become the baseline to project and monitor future performance. Benchmarks also allow measurement of member reaction to foodservice initiatives such as new menus or pricing. Most importantly, benchmarking makes supervisors more knowledgeable about their operations.

Inventories sometimes get delegated to poorly trained subordinates who miss or miscount key items. Sloppy inventories contribute to erratic cost of goods sold. Poorly organised storerooms contribute to sloppy inventories. Keys to accurate inventories include well-organised storage areas, knowledgeable individuals conducting inventories, routine and timely inventories, and organised receiving documents, invoices, and credits slips. Delegating counts is acceptable if employees are trained.

Service employees who are trained in the techniques of suggestive selling can improve your average check and bottom line. Whenever a new menu is put in place, all servers should be provided a "selling sheet" that gives key information about each entree. Such information should include cooking method, ingredients, time of preparation, and enticing descriptors to help sell each item. Just as standardised recipes are important in the kitchen for consistency of product, selling sheets provide the service staff with the knowledge and information they need to sell the product. In addition to entrees, special training should be given for the suggestive selling of appetisers, desserts, wines, and specialty alcoholic beverages.

Every month's budgeted food sales is made up of how many meals are sold and how much each guest spends on average for a meal. By breaking your projections down into meals and average check and posting your daily targets prominently in the pantry, you provide your servers with goals that connect their daily efforts to your profitability. By comparing month-to-date actual meal counts and average check to projected, you give your employees a day by day record of their progress. Most people are competitive by nature and this simple technique will become a powerful incentive to servers. The same technique can be applied to appetisers, desserts, and bottles of wine sold.

By tracking key benchmark statistics and keeping a daily log of business levels and staffing, foodservice supervisors can develop a routine system of forecasting business levels. While some level of volatility can always be expected in guest patronage, the act of forecasting, when formally done and evaluated after the fact, will assist in maintaining service levels while controlling labor cost.

While some guests are vocal with their opinions, many are not. Foodservice supervisors should make it easy for guests to provide feedback. Comment cards must be readily available, periodic surveys should be conducted, revenue benchmarks should be analysed to measure guest responses to offerings and initiatives, and employees should be trained to routinely report comments made or overheard to supervisors..

Every professional food and beverage manager is aware of these necessary elements to success. Unfortunately, in the ongoing rush of business they are often overlooked. At its root the problem is one of organisation. By taking the time to establish systems to address each guideline, by training and delegating tasks, by making each guideline part of the daily routine, each of these steps can be easily integrated into your operation. While the initial exertion may be great, so also is the ongoing payback.

Unless someone was given absolutely outstanding service or the food was just phenomenally prepared, your guests aren't going to take the time to tell you some of the things you really should know. They might tell you that the potatoes were cold or the salad was wilted, but do they ever mention how the server handled the situation? Probably not; the server is usually only mentioned as an extra in the bad scene.

That is because servers sometimes act as if everything that goes wrong is the kitchen's fault. If we really think about it, they are the last pair of eyes to see the food before it reaches the table; they should have the final say in its appearance. Servers are getting the kinds of tips they deserve for their lack of attention to guests and the details that go along with them. Your guests are giving what they think the service is worth. When they walk out your door they might tell you that the food was great, or maybe the food was a little less tasty than usual, but they will never tell you that the service was only ok or even bad.

Understand that we live in a society where it isn't ok to be confrontational and tell someone that they aren't performing well. What guests will do is tell you about the food because they never have to meet your kitchen staff. They know they may have to deal with the same server again. We don't feel like our comments are going to be heard and treated as a comment. We feel like we're going to be labeled a nasty customer and treated worse.

Most customers are forgiving and will give you another chance and return. If, however, they receive the same lack of care in service, they will quietly go away. When a server suggests wine or particular dishes and sides to go along with them, your guests don't perceive them as being pushy. On the contrary, when done in a professional manner and with some charm and class, they perceive it as great customer service! Guests may not be able to articulate these ideas to you. They just know that something is missing. Ask any businessperson who frequently dines with potential clients and he/she will tell you he/she knows the best places to take someone for smooth, seamless service.

Sanitation Risk Management (SRM) Programme

A food service organisation can be thought of as a system of basic operating activities or control points. Each control point is a miniature system with its own recognisable structure and functions. The overall success of the operation depends upon the success of each of these interrelated activities. This approach systematises the otherwise overwhelming task of managing the sanitation risks of the entire food establishment. The SRM programme inducing those risks in the course of daily operations. By thus reducing risks at each control point, managers can successful reduce the overall risks of operating a food establishment. The end result is satisfaction for guest, staff members, and owners.

Menu planning is the initial control point in the food service system. Because the menu influences the remaining control point, managers must understand all the control point before developing the menu. For example the many affects purchasing receiving storing, issuing preparing cooking and serving procedures because these procedures vary with the food products in question. The menu also affects and in some cases may be affected by the facility's design and layout equipment requirements, and labour needs. A properly designed SRM programme must begin with the menu.

Purchasing is important for maintaining the value and quality of products minimising the investment in inventory and strengthening the operation's competitive position. Sound purchasing techniques can protect profits, control costs, and reduce risks. A sound purchasing system is essential to the operation's SRM programme. Receiving is a critical control point because at this point the operation assumes ownership of the products. The receiving function involves checking quality, quantity, and price.

Proper receiving practices, when combined with skillful purchasing can maximise the benefits of a carefully planned menu. Storing serves to prevent deterioration and theft of valuable food products before the operation uses them. Food products are valuable assets that must be protected from contamination spoilage and theft in order to minimise costs and risks and maximise profits. Standards for the different types of storage (dry refrigerated, and frozen) provide this protection. Issuing is the control point at which food products are released from storage.

The objective of issuing controls is to ensure that product are only released to the production department with proper authorisation. A poorly designed issuing system can undermine an operation's sanitation efforts, increase risks and jeopardize profits. Preparing is the series of activities performed on food products before cooking cleaning and peeling vegetables, trimming meat, and assembling raw ingredients are examples of preparing activities. Food is exposed to sanitation hazards during preparing sanitation standards are therefore important at this control point.

Cooking is the control point, particularly in food service operations that prepare products well in advance of service. Menu items may be held hot or cold. Holding times should be as short as possible to maintain product quality and reduce sanitation hazards. Holding temperatures must also be monitored carefully. Serving involves physically transferring finished menu items from the production department to guests. This control point should be designed to deliver quality products to guest quickly and efficiently. Serving standards should focus on protecting good safety and quality.

Cleaning and maintenance is the final control point it is also of the most important. Cleanliness is intimately related to every other basic operating activity. Many of the standards at the other control point are standard of cleanliness and relate to sanitation and maintenance. These ten control points are the foundation of any food establishment. A comprehensive sanitation programme must address each point. Specific standards and operating procedures will vary among individual operations. However, and SRM programme based on these control point can be adapted to any food establishment.

The SRM programme is a modified version of the Hazards Analysis Critical Control Point (HACCP) approach developed jointly by the Pillsbury Company the United States Natick Laboratories and the national Aeronautics and Space Administration in 1974. The HACCP approach seeks to eliminate safety risks—primarily microbiological in food processing by identifying the specific hazards (hazard analysis) at each important point critical point in a food production system. A hazard is a biological, chemical or physical property that may cause an unacceptable consumer health risk.

A critical control point is a point or procedure in a specific food system where loss of control may result in an inacceptable health risk. A HACCP plan is a written document that delineates the formal procedures for following HACCP principles. The Food and Drug Administration's regulatory activities are conducted using the HACCP approach, for example, the FDA first applied HACCP to the low acid canned food industry. Individual hospitality organisation including Marriott, Red Lobster and Dobbs International Services, have also instituted successful HACCP programmes.

The SRM programme presented here is a HACCP based approach, which focuses on essential the ten control points common to most food establishments. Standards and procedures for each control point are presented as they relate to the four resource under a managers control inventory people equipment, and facilities. A resource evaluation is necessary for each of the ten- control point. The result is a systematic approach to managing risks.

Inventory is an essential management resource because it is converted into revenue and ultimately into profits. Inventory in a food service operation normally consists of food products, beverage and non-food items such as linens and cleaning chemicals. Inventory control is a vital link in an operation cost and quality control systems. Inventory items are assets which must be protected from spoilage, contamination pilferage, and waste. Because the hospitality industry is labour-intensive that is it relies on large staff people are an important resource. It is managements responsibility to train staff members in proper sanitation practices.

Failing to control this important resource undermines the SRM programme and jeopardizes the establishment's bottom line. The food establishment equipment represents a substantial investment. Equipment selection is important to the SRM programme, as is the proper cleaning and maintenance of each piece of equipment. A food service operation's facilities also represent a sizable investment, and their design and layout have a great impact on the success of the SRM programme.

Benefits of the SRM Programme

A formalised SRM programme ensures a continuous effort toward better sanitation. It guarantees that important points are not overlooked or forgotten in the course of daily operations and personnel changes. Naturally, a comprehensive SRM programme costs money. However, it provides an immediate payback to the business by performing the following functions

— Meeting guest expectations upon which the establishment's success depends

— Protecting guest and staff health thereby reducing staff member absences

— Reducing the operations liability for accident injuries or death

— Increasing the useful life of the operation facilities and equipment

— Increasing the effectiveness and reducing the cot of cleaning and sanitization procedures with the proper use of chemicals.

- — Reducing the risks associated with the storage and application of toxic chemical by standardising products and procedures.
- — Simplifying supervision with the use of checklists
- — Eliminating product waste and simplifying work methods through the use of written cleaning procedures
- — Establishing management objectives which can be used to measure the progress of the business toward reducing risks.
- — Providing an acceptable return on investment for the owners for the business
- — Reducing the risks of operating a food establishment.

As this list of benefit including, a comprehensive SRM programme does not cost as much as it pays. However, the return on this investment depends on how well management communities the SRM standards and how well everyone performs to uphold these standards. Management must make sanitation part of daily operation and make all staff members aware of its importance.

11

WASTE PREVENTION

Protecting the nature is one of the many challenges that hotel and motel operators face. Hotels and motels can use their own resources better, spend less time and money managing waste, and, at the same time, play a significant educational role for their guests. Waste prevention is a win-win approach that is neither costly nor cumbersome. It is also the approach that tops the list of solid waste management options adopted by the US Environmental Protection Agency, followed by (in order of desirability) recycling (including composting), incineration, and landfill disposal. Unlike all the other strategies, waste prevention decreases the amount (and toxicity) of waste generated.

Prevention also reduces the cost of collection, recycling, and disposal systems, and it helps alleviate the political conflicts that often surround waste management systems. The growth of recycling during the 1980s and 1990s represents a step forward in the management of materials, because recycling mines the waste stream for valuable materials that can be reprocessed into new products. But waste prevention—including the reuse of products—is even more basic. It avoids the creation of waste in the first place.

Solid Waste

In recent years, waste as the visible result of the inefficient use of natural resources. Products and packages with short life cycles (including those considered "disposable") create problems that go far beyond disposal. Short-lived products also contribute to the depletion of natural resources and to the creation of pollution during materials extraction, product manufacture, and product use. Once discarded, products and packaging impose substantial environmental and economic burdens on the nation.

Solutions for Waste Prevention

Simply defined, waste prevention is a reduction in the amount and/or toxicity of materials entering the waste stream prior to recycling, treatment, or disposal. "Source reduction"—that is, reducing waste at the source—is another term for this approach. Waste prevention can be part of an "environmentally sustainable" way of living and doing business meaning it can be sustained long-term in harmony with the environment, without depleting limited resources and without polluting our air, land, or water.

Waste prevention is a winning strategy, both environmentally and economically. It can be accomplished in a variety of ways. Waste prevention may mean a change in practices to encourage the use of durable, repairable, and reusable products. It may mean changing a product or package to reduce the materials needed to make that product or package. Or it may even mean eliminating the need for a specific product or certain packaging elements.

Strategies that prevent waste also conserve valuable resources. For example, reusing corrugated boxes—the largest-volume component of a hotel's waste stream—reduces raw material use, avoids the need for energy to manufacture or recycle boxes, and prevents the pollution that arises from the manufacture and recycling of additional boxes. Waste prevention is a call to do more with less. Making this transition will require:

— Fundamental changes in the design and use of products and packages and in systems for distributing them

— Essential shifts in business, institutional, and individual practices to achieve more efficient materials use

— Public and private promotion of waste reduction and careful resource use by communities and businesses.

It is difficult to estimate the amount of solid waste generated by individual hotels. However, critical factors include the number of employees, the number of guest rooms, the scope of kitchen and restaurant services, and the size and number of meeting rooms or convention facilities. Luxury hotels usually employ more staff and offer more services to guests than more moderately priced properties, and thus often generate more waste. Two categories of garbage dominate the typical hotel waste stream: paper and food/organics.

Starting a comprehensive waste prevention programme is a team effort, It requires planning, communication with all employees and departments, and the development of well-understood goals. To get started, hotels and motels can target their waste prevention initiatives by looking in three key directions:

— Assessing purchasing decisions

— Understanding how materials and equipment are used

— Examining the waste stream.

Assessing purchasing decisions: Since most products purchased eventually end up in the hotel's waste stream, a purchasing assessment can determine if longer-lasting, repairable, and reusable items could replace shorter-lived, non-repairable, single-use products. Purchasing plays an especially important role in waste prevention. Simply, if an item is not bought, it cannot be thrown away. Incorporating waste prevention objectives into purchasing policies can decrease the amount of waste generated, encourage vendors to develop and sell products that create less waste, and often save money. Keep in mind that hotels—like other businesses—pay for the use of items twice: once upon purchase and again at disposal.

To explore the role purchasing can play in waste prevention, each purchasing agent or general manager could begin by asking, for each item delivered, why do we have this? If an item is not deemed essential, why buy it? If it is needed, does the product chosen make the most economical use of materials and offer the least possible toxicity? Do vendors sell less harmful alternatives? Can the property buy the product in bulk to reduce costs and packaging waste? Buying products in the largest quantity possible in one package utilizes less packaging per ounce than several smaller containers. Can containers be returned for reuse, or can they be recycled?

Understanding how materials and equipment are used: Besides procurement, hotels can prevent waste by changing the way they use products and materials. For example, circulating a memo to five people instead of distributing separate copies to each person saves four copies; using electronic mail saves six copies, including the original. Hotels can also "intensify" their use of products to keep them in working condition longer and to get the maximum use out of a product.

For instance, by repairing broken guest room furniture, office equipment, and kitchen appliances, hotels can lengthen the useful life of these products, keeping them out of the waste stream longer and saving money, too. In addition, hotels can reuse materials from one area in other parts of the property—eliminating the need to buy, use, and dispose of additional items—or they can donate them to charity.

Examining the waste stream: The goal of examining a property's waste stream is to look for opportunities to prevent waste by identifying materials that are:

— Major components of the waste stream (for example, office paper)

— Easy to reduce (for example, by composting landscaping waste)

— Sources of pollution in the local waste management system (for example, batteries).

To learn what materials make up a hotel's waste stream—and the cost of handling them—a hotel could undertake any or all of the following activities:

— A visual inspection of the hotel, conducted by walking through various parts of the property, including guest rooms, food service areas, offices, and loading docks

— Interviews with staff in each area, including grounds crews, housekeeping staff, office personnel, and food service workers

— Examination of purchasing records

— Sorting of waste by department (or hotel-wide); in "dumpster diving," "divers" physically separate and measure materials discarded in dumpsters and recycling bins

— An examination of waste hauling records to learn the weight or volume of waste generated and the cost of disposing of or recycling that waste By gathering quantitative information on discarded materials, hotels can set realistic goals for preventing waste.

Balancing waste prevention with service and ratings. Waste prevention does not have to mean a reduction in the level of service offered, even for the most luxurious hotel. In many cases, waste prevention can be an "invisible" strategy, one that takes place behind the scenes of a hotel's public operations. However, other strategies may be more visible—for example, using refillable shampoo dispensers instead of mini-sized bottles—and managers may be concerned that their guests will perceive the change as a cut in service. Yet there are many ways to make guests feel pampered without contributing to the waste stream.

Some luxury hotels have been able to use the money saved by purchasing refillable or reusable products to offer higher quality products overall, such as betterquality shampoos in the refillable dispensers. Hotels might offer guests a glass of champagne upon arrival, fresh flowers in the room, or a basket of fruit. Managers may also be concerned that some waste prevention measures could lower the ratings the property receives from independent travel organisations. According to representatives of Mobil Travel Guide and the American Automobile Association's (AAA) Industry Evaluations department—the two leading sources of these ratings—this is not necessarily the case.

Hotel evaluations are based on the overall level of service a property provides, so presentation counts, along with the specific items presented. At the same time, hotel inspectors may evaluate certain changes as a cut in service—regardless of their presentation. Representatives of AAA point out that hotel managers can contact their inspectors to discuss the implementation of waste prevention measures at their properties.

Mobil Travel Guide does not rely on a checklist or set criteria regarding the specific nature of the items or services a hotel must supply in order to be awarded a top rating. A marketing approach. Indeed, some hotels have found that their guests appreciate those steps taken to help the environment. Educating guests about a hotel or motel's policies and asking for feedback can be an important part of a hotel's marketing approach.

Guests who have become used to "green" habits in their own homes may appreciate a door-hanger that allows them to decide whether or not to have newspapers delivered or sheets changed daily throughout their visit. Properties that cater especially to families might choose to educate and involve their guests in waste prevention, while businessoriented properties might opt for a more subtle approach. Individual managers can determine how to balance waste prevention with the level of convenience and comfort their guests have come to expect.

Waste Prevention Strategies in Hotel and Motel

Within a hotel or motel, each functional area presents its own set of waste prevention challenges. The list below, which suggests a variety of specific strategies for preventing waste, is organised according to these functional areas.

Guest Rooms

— Review policies for guest room amenities and the packaging of those items. Inform guests of efforts to provide amenities that have less impact on the environment.

— Provide soap, shampoo, and lotion in refillable dispensers, instead of individual containers. Provide individual containers only upon request.

— Do not remove "gift" amenities from the room after a guest departs unless the seal on the package is broken. Leave unopened amenities in the room for the next guest.

— Reduce size of individually packaged items, such as bar soap, to reduce the quantities left over.

— Rather than offering individually packaged amenities, consider offering another type of gift, such as a basket of fruit or a bottle of wine.

— Wait to replace-half-filled toilet paper rolls and tissue boxes until they are almost completely used. Leave new rolls and tissue boxes in bathrooms for guests to replace.

— If half-used items must be removed, place them in employee rest rooms or donate them to charity.

— Give newpapers, shoeshine kits, and showercaps to guests only upon request. To avoid delivering newspapers to guests who don't want them, provide guests with a door hanger that allows them to request the next morning's papers.

— Deliver newspapers to guest rooms without plastic bag wrappings.

— Provide guest rooms with unwrapped, reusable drinking glasses and coffee cups. Check with the local health department about storing glasses upside down on trays, rather than using disposable paper covers.

— Eliminate the use of plastic liners in ice buckets.

— Eliminate the use of paper doilies and paper tray covers,

— Reduce printed information placed in rooms. Condense printed material where possible or designate a special television channel for hotel information.

— Order only as many telephone directories as the number of rooms and phones. Directory distributors often deliver many more copies than are needed.

Laundry and Housekeeping

1. *Laundry and Dry Cleaning*

- Ask guests whether they would like to have their towels and sheets replaced daily, or whether they want to "help the environment" by reusing them. Besides saving water and energy, reduced laundering will also reduce the use of detergent and bleach. Make sure guest bathrooms have enough towel-rail space to hang wet towels.
- After dry cleaning, return clothes in reusable garment bags to eliminate the need for single-use plastic bags.
- Offer plastic wrap for dry cleaned clothing only upon request.
- Eliminate cardboard backing for laundered shirts.
- Reuse wire clothes hangers from guest drycleaning services for guest bathrobes and employee uniforms or return them to vendors.

2. *Resing Textiles*

- Convert damaged textiles, such as uniforms and linens, into useful items. For example, it's possible to turn torn bed sheets, towels, and banquet linens into reusable guest-room laundry bags, baby bibs, crib bumper pads, aprons, cleaning rags, and bar covers. Another possibility: repair torn bed linen and reuse it on smaller cots or cribs.
- Replace single-use items with reusable items such as napkins, tablecloths, and hand towels. When they are worn, turn them into cleaning rags.
- Dye stained towels a darker color for reuse at the pool or beach, or as cleaning cloths.
- Extend the useful life of draperies by, rotating them to expose different portions to sunlight.

3. *Cleaning Products*

- Buy cleaning products in bulk and in concentrated form, because one large container of product uses less packaging per ounce than several smaller containers. At the same time, order only what can be used before the product expires.

— Install mixing stations in the housekeeping department to reduce spiliage. Educate staff on proper mixing of concentrates to avoid waste and save money.

— Fill smaller reusable containers with cleaning products from larger containers.

— Use refillable pump spray bottles that can be reused instead of single-use aerosol cans.

— Buy cleaning products that are biodegradable.

— Buy supplies from vendors who take back the containers in which they ship cleaning materials

— Clean and reuse dustmop heads.

— Use reusable vacuum cleaner bags.

4. *Reducing the Use of Toxic Chemicals*

— Minimise the use of products that contain toxic chemicals. The types of products that may pose toxic risks include pesticides, herbicides, bleaches, oven cleaners, drain cleaners, acids, disinfectants, general cleaning chemicals, caustic cleaners, window cleaners, solvents, paints, adhesives, fuels, oils and grease, and hydraulic fluids. Begin by identifying where toxic chemicals are being used and the reason for their use. Review handling, storage, and disposal procedures and compile a record of toxic materials use. Where possible, identify, test, and use environmentally preferable alternatives.

— With the approval of the hotel's engineer, use a plunger or a snake rather than chemical solutions to remove plumbing obstructions, as long as the hotel's pipes are not in fragile condition. This avoids deleterious effects on waterways from the use of chemicals.

— Reduce the need for pesticide applications in guest rooms and employee work areas by making these areas less attractive to crawling pests. Remove food containers, garbage, and recycling containers frequently; clean employee break rooms daily; and report cracks around doors and windows to the engineering department.

— Check labels on room deodorizers for hazardous chemical content.

— Deodorizers are often used to mask smoke and mildew odors. Reduce the need for these products by: cleaning air conditioner coils and changing air conditioner filters regularly; sealing cracks around windows, doors, and air conditioning units; and operating air conditioners at temperatures recommended by the engineering department.

— Check buckets, cans, drums, and other chemical containers periodically and replace leaky ones.

— Use a containment pan at all times to prevent the leaching of unused chemicals, such as cleaning chemicals, oils, grease, and caustic cleaners.

— Clean chemical leaks and spills immediately.

— Store unused chemicals in a cool, dry, and well-ventilated place.

— Dispose of chemicals according to label instructions.

— Use rechargeable batteries wherever possible.

— Collect old alkaline, dry cell, and worn-out rechargeable batteries used in hotel walkie-talkies and pagers at a central collection point and dispose of them in accordance with local requirements. Many municipalities have special rules for disposing of batteries, and some locales have battery collection programmes. Batteries may contain toxic chemicals. If they are disposed of with other garbage, they may enter landfills, garbage incinerators, home septic systems, or public sewer systems. From there they can move into air, land, and water, where they may affect public health and the environment.

Food and Beverage Service

Food Preparation

— Buy locally grown food, especially organically grown items. This avoids the pollution associated with transportation and pesticides and provides guests with the freshest foods in season.

— Plan menus so that fresh ingredients are interchangeable among recipes. In this way, produce and other perishable foods can be used up in different recipes—not wasted if guests order less of a particular dish.

— Reassess portion sizes to minimise the amount of foods that patrons leave on their plates, as current specifications may be unnecessarily wasteful and expensive. Customising portion sizes may require buying uncut foods (including meat, produce, and other products) rather than buying foods that are already cut-to-size and ready-to-use.

— To reduce food waste, offer guests the option of ordering half-portions. Prepare smaller portions of precooked foods (pasta, potatoes, vegetables) to reduce the amount later discarded.

— Purchase foods in bulk and store unused portions in airtight reusable food containers. Buying products in the largest quantity possible in one package uses less packaging per ounce than several smaller containers. But buy only what can be used. Overpurchasing can result in spoilage, defeating the purpose of buying in bulk.

— Ask suppliers to ship goods, such as milk, bread, meats, fish, and produce, in reusable shipping containers that can be returned to the supplier.

— To reduce the amount of food that must be discarded from salad bars, set up salad bar offerings in smaller containers and replenish them more often.

— Use scraps left over from food preparation to make soups and stocks for donation.

— Donate edible, unused food to local charities. More than 100 programmes throughout the United States accept prepared food—packaged, prepared, fresh, frozen, or baked—that restaurants and hotels can no longer use. Donor programmes deliver food to soup kitchens, homeless shelters, senior citizens' programmes, day-care centers, and food pantries. Foodchain, an Atlanta-based national coalition of prepared and perishable food programmes, publishes Fighting Hunger with Prepared and Perishable Food and will advise those interested in starting a programme.

— If possible, collect unusable food scraps and arrange to have them picked up by local pig farmers for use as animal feed. First, check with the local health department or cooperative extension office, as some states and municipalities do not allow the feeding of food scraps to swine.

— Arrange for a renderer to collect and recycle cooking fat, grease, and bones.

— Install filters that extend the life of deep frying cooking oil. Without filtration, oil becomes contaminated with food particles more quickly.

— Compost kitchen scraps and food waste. Like landscaping waste, the compost resulting from food waste can be used in landscaping as a soil amendment.

Food service items

— Use reusable plastic lids or reusable and recyclable aluminum foil to cover food in coolers and steam tables.

— Rinse and reuse pieces of aluminum foil that were used to cover pans of food.

— Replace individual condiment packages with bulk dispensers in restaurants and employee cafeterias. Review health regulations first; some local codes allow dispensers in employee cafeterias but prohibit their use in public restaurants.

— Avoid individually wrapped packages of sugar, butter, jam, etc.

— Use dispensers or small dishes, instead of prepackaged containers.

— For take-out orders, offer condiments, napkins, and straws upon request instead of allowing customers to help themselves.

— For employee cafeterias and room service delivery, replace disposable items with washable, reusable plates, trays, and utensils, and reduce unnecessary packaging.

— Use reusable linen napkins instead of paper for all food service, including employee cafeterias and room service. Where paper must be used, install napkin dispensers and buy smaller sizes.

— Use washable hats and aprons for kitchen staff instead of dispos-able paper ones.

— Use cloth rags and sponges to wipe spills in the kitchen and on dining room tables instead of paper towels. Use stained wash cloths and towels for cleaning.

— Use spun glass pads for scrubbing pots and pans instead of steel wool scouring pads. This new type of pad comes either soaped or unsoaped. They last longer than steel pads and do not rust.

— Reduce menu printing costs wherever possible, for example, by reusing menus, eliminating paper inserts, and using boards to post daily specials.

— Recover mistakenly discarded items from the garbage, such as flatware, plates, linen napkins, and towels.

— Install a magnet on food waste containers to recover flatware accidentally thrown away with food waste. o Inspect food service equipment for leaks and malfunctions and repair or replace as needed.

— Avoid using cellophane wrap for fruit baskets and gifts delivered to guest rooms.

Beverage service

— Use fountains to dispense soda.

— Offer draft beer.

— Purchase milk in large (five gallon) plastic dispenser bags, delivered in reusable crates, rather than buying milk by the gallon or in difficult-to-recycle coated cardboard cartons.

— Serve milk from steel dispensers to decrease use of single-use containers. Use refillable beverage containers, especially for room service and in restaurants and bars, where collection of empty bottles is easily controlled. Replace cocktail napkins with permanent coasters at dining room tables and bars.

— Avoid using doilies and frilled toothpicks for beverages. Replace toothpicks and disposable cocktail stirrers with reusable plastic stirrers (if approved by local and state health departments).

— Use reusable metal or nylon coffee filters.

Offices

Avoiding paper use

— Before printing, confirm whether a paper copy is needed.

— Use electronic mail and voice mail instead of paper copies.

— Evaluate internal reporting paperwork and eliminate obsolete or unnecessary forms.

— Post office-wide announcements on a bulletin board or in a binder instead of giving a copy to each employee.

— Store files on reusable computer disks instead of in hard copy form.

— Eliminate fax cover sheets.

Preventing office paper waste

— To reduce paper use, route documents electronically when information must be shared internally.

— Edit and proofread documents on computer screens before printing.

— Prepare documents in double-sided and single-spaced formats.

— Adjust document margins to avoid pages with little text.

— Load laser printer paper trays with paper already used on one side for drafts and internal memos.

— Use paper already used on one side for drafts and notes.

— Programme photocopying machines to automatically make doublesided copies.

— Post signs by photocopiers to instruct and remind staff.

— Make only as many copies as you need.

— Set up central filing systems to avoid filing identical documents in individual filing cabinets.

— Use small pieces of paper for short memos.

Publications and mailings

— Eliminate subscriptions to newspapers and magazines that go unread. Circulate and share documents, publications, and telephone books.

— Reduce unwanted direct mail by asking vendors to remove your name from their mailing lists. Ask vendors not to sell or trade your name to other direct mail companies,

— For hotel mailings, target direct-mail recipients as precisely as pos-sible to reduce the number of pieces sent. Eliminate duplication by frequently updating mailing lists.

— Request address corrections on correspondence. You will save postage and labor costs as well.

— Send bills in two-way envelopes.

Office supplies and equipment

a) Buy reusable items instead of single-use items, such as:

— refillable pens and pencils
— refillable laser toner printer cartridges
— multistrike typewriter ribbons
— envelopes with metal clasps
— erasable wall calendars.

b) Buy sturdy, long-lasting office supplies such as staplers, scissors, file holders, and book ends.

c) Adopt strategies that promote paper waste reduction, such as buying or leasing:
— copying machines and laser printers that can make double-sided copies
— computer software that permits faxing directly from a computer to avoid unnecessary print-outs
— electronic mail systems
— fax machines that use plain paper.

d) Reuse file folders.

e) Use interoffice envelopes and folders that can be used many times for routing in-house mail and correspondence.

Conference Facilities

Develop a brochure for conference planners that encourages exhibitors and attendees to:

— print their materials on both sides of the page 1 produce printed materials in limited quantities with only a 10-to-15 percent buffer

a) instead of handing out large conference packets, offer conference literature on a table so attendees can take only those items they wish to keep

b) take back excess promotional materials

c) use paper compatible with the hotel's recycling programme

— Offer incentives such as reduced disposal fees or faster breakdown services to convention exhibitors who minimise leftovers and take back excess materials.

— Use reusable cloth drapes or skirts on display booths rather than single-use varieties.

— Reuse pens, pencils, and name tag holders. Place clearly marked collection boxes at conference room exits and post signs to inform conference attendees of the policy.

— Supply note pads with limited sheets in conference areas and guest rooms. After conferences, use the blank portions of the pads as scrap paper in hotel offices. Or donate blank portions of pads to schools or local charities.

— Provide reusable drinking glasses and coffee cups.

— To avoid the use of individual cream and sugar packets, provide cream for coffee or tea in insulated or chilled pitchers and provide sugar in dispensers.

— For special events, ask florists to rent potted floral arrangements that can be returned after events. If unable to rent them, reuse the purchased ones for other hotel events or place them in lobby or food service areas.

— For banquets, holiday celebrations, and other catered functions, encourage guests and employees to take table decorations home. Or reuse them in other areas of the hotel.

Maintenance

Equipment

— Develop a preventive maintenance programme and ensure that equipment is operating efficiently.

— Operate and maintain equipment according to manufacturer's recommendations to extend equipment life and maximise productivity.

— Use high-mileage tires on vehicles.

— Keep tires filled to proper air pressure, thereby maximising their life.

— Have truck and passenger vehicle tires retreaded, instead of purchasing new ones.

— Use re-refined lubricating oil.

— Install reusable furnace and air conditioner filters. Reusable filters have removable material that can be washed and returned to the frame for further use.

Paint

— Purchase paint in the amount that is needed at the time. Buy paint for touch-ups in small quantities, otherwise it often ends up discarded later.

— Instead of oil-based paint, use less toxic water-based paint.

— Use leftover paint for other projects. Remix and reuse paint where possible. Where no use can be found on-site, donate paint to charitable groups.

— When discarding paints, review disposal practices and identify environmentally sound solutions. Paints are usually characterised as hazardous waste and as such require special disposal procedures. Contact your local solid waste office for details on disposal options.

Landscaping

— Leave grass clippings on the lawn or mulch grass and leaves. If the lawn is cut regularly, clippings should be small enough to fall between the standing blades; as they decompose they become a good fertilizer. It is unlikely that anyone will notice that clippings have not been raked and bagged.

— Compost yard waste on site. Check local regulations: in some locales, it's possible to compost some food wastes as well.

— Offer live plants slated for replacement to employees or donate them.

— Practice xeriscaping. Xeriscaping includes growing drought-tolerant plants in desert areas, growing lawns only where practical—thereby reducing grass clippings—and planting lower-maintenance shrubs and bushes that require less-frequent cutting and pruning, generating smaller quantities of yard waste.

— Return plastic seedling pots to nurseries.

— Use large tree limbs for firewood or donate them.

— After pruning trees, chop smaller pieces of wood into chips and use as mulch.

— Minimise the use of toxic pesticides. An alternative is to practice integrated pest management, which controls pests through the judicious use of pesticides in combination with other techniques, including biological and mechanical methods.

— Minimise the use of toxic herbicides and fertilizers.

Remodeling and Construction

— When remodeling or replacing items, such as carpeting, use the older items in another part of the property or donate them to charity.

— Incorporate used and recycled items in construction projects, including building materials, cabinetry, doors, and fixtures.

— If storage room permits, keep excess materials on hand for repair projects.

— Refinish and reupholster damaged and out-of-style furniture.

— Dye linens and carpet to match renovated facilities, instead of purchasing new items or redecorating from scratch.

Building specifications

— In evaluating building plans, give careful consideration to efficient use of materials.

— To avoid overbuying, establish strict estimating procedures to ensure that materials are purchased in correct quantities. Order materials to be consistent with room dimensions. For example, wallboard is available in a number of stock sizes and can be ordered to fit custom designs.

— Ask vendors to help identify building materials with reduced toxic content.

— Use kiln-dried wood lumber to reduce waste from on-site war-page and shrinkage.

— Use steel studs for framing rather than wood. Steel studs are made from recycled steel and are recyclable. In addition, they last longer than wood, as they do not rot and are not susceptible to termite damage.

— Reduce the loss of building materials to weather and other damage. For example, use plastic to cover bags of mortar, stack blocks and bricks carefully to keep them from getting lost in the mud, and keep lumber covered and off the ground. Centralise wood cutting to make maximum use of off-cuts. This reduces the need to cut full-length lumber for small pieces.

— Use standard size building materials (such as eight-foot lengths) to reduce non-standard size off-cuts of lumber and wallboard.

— Ask suppliers to take back or buy back unusable or rejected materials. Ask suppliers to remove packaging before shipping materials to the work site, to wrap materials in reusable blankets, and to backhaul shipping containers and pallets.

— To give contractors an incentive to produce less waste, require them to include the cost of removing construction waste in their bids.

— Use carpet tacks instead of floor-covering adhesives, which usually contain toxic ingredients.

— Use reclaimed (remixed) latex (water-based) paints.

— Reuse broken concrete for erosion control.

Purchasing

— Review buying habits and purchase only what is needed.

— Chart the shelf life of items and purchase only when the item is needed. This reduces spoilage.

— Buy for quality and durability, simplicity and repairability.

Changing purchasing practices

— Establish standards or guidelines for what is purchased.

— Work with vendors to procure products that promote waste prevention.

— Vendors may be able to change products and packaging to reduce the waste the hotel must manage. For example, ask food service vendors if they can deliver items in reusable shipping containers.

— Notify vendors of your efforts to obtain products and services that have less impact on the environment. Ask vendors about their products and practices; patronize suppliers who have made changes in products and packaging.

— Combine supply orders from various departments. More packaging waste is created with multiple smaller orders. Also, hotels that make purchases on a decentralised basis cannot benefit from volume purchasing discounts.

— Rent items or equipment that are rarely used, rather than buying them.

— Repair items rather than purchasing new ones.

— Buy or lease used or remanufactured furniture, fixtures, and equipment. Typical remanufacturing operations performed by suppliers are replacement of worn parts, refinishing of metal or wooden surfaces, repair of scratches, dents, and holes, and reupholstering of cushions. Extending the life of furniture, fixtures, and equipment through remanufacturing reduces the rate at which they are discarded as waste.

— Buy products with recycled content to help conserve natural resources.

Choosing products

Where necessary, pay a little more and buy reusable, refillable, durable, and repairable products and equipment. Over the useful life of the item, buying for durability and reuse will save money; keeping materials in use longer will generate less waste to be managed.

— Negotiate for longer and more comprehensive warranties and service contracts when purchasing durable products.

— Instead of buying new mattresses, have older ones remanufactured. This process reuses the steel frame and structural sections of the mattress, while replacing the cushioning and cloth sections.

— Purchase sheets with a high thread count for longer wear.

— Provide reusable mugs for staff instead of disposable paper or polystyrene cups.

— Donate items to charitable organisations for reuse when purchasing new items. Donations could include linens, blankets, and old curtains that are no longer being used, but are still in good condition.

— Usable goods may also include china and glassware, furniture, lamps, uniforms, and lost-and-found items.

— For toxic materials, review whether their use is necessary, how frequently they are used, storage instructions, container disposal, recyclability, and reuse options. Look for less-toxic alternatives.

— Replace disposable batteries with rechargeable batteries in pagers, walkie-talkies, radios, calculators and flashlights. This reduces the amount of lead acid batteries in landfills (lead is the leading toxic substance in landfills).

Packaging

— Choose packages that use less material. Avoid those that use several layers of packaging when fewer would do.

— Certain industries can tailor their packaging, in ways specific to that industry, to reduce overall packaging use. Ask vendors which packaging options are available to you. For example, beer can be packaged in kegs, in bottles—either refillable or single-use—or in cans; in flats or in boxes; with plastic collars or without; and with or without stretchwrap, among other options. Analyse the waste implications of each option and find out if your vendors can package supplies differently.

— Buy products in the largest quantity possible in one package. One large container of product utilises less packaging per ounce than several smaller containers. Ordering in bulk for items such as cleaning products, food products, and office supplies reduces packaging waste and saves time, energy, and money.

— Ask vendors to increase the case size of certain items so that fewer cases are needed for the same number of items.

— Work with vendors to schedule deliveries so that supplies can be immediately unpacked and packing materials returned to suppliers for reuse.

— Ask suppliers to take back shipping pallets. If they cannot, reuse them on site or sell or donate them.

— Reuse packing materials, such as boxes, shipping peanuts, and bubble wrap for outgoing shipments. Or make them available to a local mailing firm.

12

EFFECTIVE HOUSEKEEPING

Housekeeping, reception, porters, cleaning, room service, restaurant, bar, the list of departments is long enough, but each department has several grades of staff. The Housekeeping department must be the most important. It has the greatest proportion of staffing hours to cover, the most staff, the most hours to cover and it is a cost center. Unlike the restaurant and bar, which are revenue centers, and as long as they are not overstaffed, the more staff you have the more revenue is generated. The housekeeping department is also the one the customers notice most if anything is wrong. You have to have the right number of staff on duty, or it shows. The housekeeping department can have the following staff depending on the size of hotel.

Housekeeper and assistant housekeepers, room maids, cleaners, staffmaids, cloakroom attendants, houseporters, valets, laundry and linen keeper. The staff hours of cover depend on the hotel and type of customer, business people require different time schedules to people on holiday with children. The staff need to be scheduled accordingly and in a ratio to the number of guests staying in the hotel. Fortunately, most people book ahead and the workload is known well in advance, especially during peak periods.

Your staffing requirement will depend on the occupancy of your hotel. It is possible to get quite good estimates of staff numbers based on average times to do tasks, such as cleaning a room. Then you can allocate 10, or 15, or even 20 rooms to each room maid. It is also quite easy to estimate the total number of staff needed in a year for a task. For example, cleaning an occupied room takes 30mins/day, en-suite bathroom 6mins/day, therefore a maid for every 13 occupied rooms. A hotel with 100 rooms needs 8 maids. Then we can sum this up for a year of 365 days, which comes to 2900 maid days per year. We can then divide this by the number of days a maid works per year, say 240, and arrive at a figure of 12 full time maids.

Visual Rota is a computer programme design for staff scheduling. You can use Visual Rota to allocate training days for new staff and existing, or keep records of sickness, absenteeism, lateness, frequency of requests and holidays. An existing hotel will be using their established working practice for staffing. Visual Rota enables you to analyse this and see if improvements can be made and how much you can save by changing your working practice. Staff need an incentive to change and if you offer part of your savings as a pay increase, that goes a long way to getting the changes accepted.

Visual Rota enables you to move your staff around to minimise the effects of peaks and troughs in occupancy levels. You can bring in more staff when needed and give them days off during slack periods. The programme keeps track of their hours and shifts, so everyone gets exactly the right number of hours of work, but your costs are minimised. Other departments are equally capable of being analysed and scheduled by Visual Rota. It is possible to have one file for the entire hotel, or several files to cover each area, floor or department. Whichever method you use at the moment, you can do the same on the computer, but faster.

There is always a compromise between the number of staff doing a particular job and the cover they provide. If there is only one housekeeper, then the maximum cover would be 40 hours/week, whilst the staff rota would be providing up to 168 hours of cover a week, hence one of the main management functions is to determine how much staffing is provided and at what grade of staff. Fortunately, hoteliers are not subject to staffing levels determined by legislation, and can decide for themselves.

An intelligent housekeeper will be better able to judge of the average consumption of each article by the household; and if that quantity be, at any time, exceeded, the cause may be discovered and rectified, if it proceed from waste or carelessness. Although in the department of the cook, the housekeeper does not generally much interfere, yet it is necessary that she should possess a good knowledge of the culinary art, as, in many instances, it may be requisite for her to take the superintendence of the kitchen.

As a rule, it may be stated, that the housekeeper, in those establishments where there is no house steward or man cook, undertakes the preparation of the confectionary, attends to the preserving and pickling of fruits and vegetables; and, in a general way, to the more difficult branches of the art of cookery. Much of these arrangements will depend, however, on the qualifications of the cook; for instance, if she be an able artiste, there will be but little necessity for the housekeeper to interfere, except in the already noticed articles of confectionary, etc.

On the contrary, if the cook be not so clever an adept in her art, then it will be requisite for the housekeeper to give more of her attention to the business of the kitchen, than in the former case. It will be one of the duties of the housekeeper to attend to the marketing, in the absence of either a house steward or man cook. The daily duties of a housekeeper are regulated, in a great measure, by the extent of the establishment she superintends.After breakfast, which, in large establishments, she will take in the "housekeeper's room" with the lady's-maid, butler, and valet, and where they will be waited on by the still-room maid, she will, on various days set apart for each purpose, carefully examine the household linen, with a view to its being repaired, or to a further quantity being put in hand to be made.

The housekeeper's room is generally made use of by the lady's-maid, butler, and valet, who take there their breakfast, tea, and supper. The lady's-maid will also use this apartment as a sitting-room, when not engaged with her lady, or with some other duties, which would call her elsewhere. In different establishments, according to their size and the rank of the family, different rules of course prevail. For instance, in the mansions of those of very high rank, and where there is a house steward, there are two distinct tables kept, one in the steward's room for the principal members of the household, the other in the servants' hall, for the other domestics. At the steward's dinner-table, the steward and housekeeper preside; and here, also, are present the lady's-maid, butler, valet, and head gardener.

After dinner, the housekeeper, having seen that all the members of the establishment have regularly returned to their various duties, and that all the departments of the household are in proper working order, will have many important matters claiming her attention. She will, possibly, have to give the finishing touch to some article of confectionary, or be occupied with some of the more elaborate processes of the still-room. There may also be the dessert to arrange, ice-creams to make; and all these employments call for no ordinary degree of care, taste, and attention. The still-room was formerly much more in vogue than at present; for in days of "auld lang syne," the still was in constant requisition for the supply of sweet-flavoured waters for the purposes of cookery, scents and aromatic substances used in the preparation of the toilet, and cordials in cases of accidents and illness. There are some establishments, however, in which distillation is still carried on, and in these, the still-room maid has her old duties to perform.

In a general way, however, this domestic is immediately concerned with the housekeeper. For the latter she lights the fire, dusts her room, prepares the breakfast-table, and waits at the different meals taken in the housekeeper's room. A still-room maid may learn a very great deal of useful knowledge from her intimate connection with the housekeeper, and if she be active and intelligent, may soon fit herself for a better position in the household. In the evening, the housekeeper will often busy herself with the necessary preparations for the next day's duties. Numberless small, but still important arrangements, will have to be made, so that everything may move smoothly.

In a physical point of view, a housekeeper should be healthy and strong, and be particularly clean in her person, and her hands, although they may show a degree of roughness, from the nature of some of her employments, yet should have a nice inviting appearance. In her dealings with the various tradesmen, and in her behaviour to the domestics under her, the demeanour and conduct of the housekeeper should be such as, in neither case, to diminish, by an undue familiarity, her authority or influence. As, in the winter months, servants have much more to do, in consequence of the necessity there is to attend to the number of fires throughout the household, not much more than the ordinary every-day work can be attempted.

The spring is the usual period set apart for house-cleaning, and removing all the dust and dirt, which will necessarily, with the best of housewives, accumulate during the winter months, from the smoke of the coal, oil, gas, etc. This season is also well adapted for washing and bleaching linen, etc., as, the weather, not being then too hot for the exertions necessary in washing counterpanes, blankets, and heavy things in general, the work is better and more easily done than in the intense heats of July, which month some recommend for these purposes.

Winter curtains should be taken down, and replaced by the summer white ones; and furs and woollen cloths also carefully laid by. The former should be well shaken and brushed, and then pinned upon paper or linen, with camphor to preserve them from the moths. Furs, etc., will be preserved in the same way. Included, under the general description of house-cleaning, must be understood, turning out all the nooks and corners of drawers, cupboards, lumber-rooms, lofts, etc., with a view of getting rid of all unnecessary articles, which only create dirt and attract vermin; sweeping of chimneys, taking up carpets, painting and whitewashing the kitchen and offices, papering rooms, when needed, and, generally speaking, the house putting on, with the approaching summer, a bright appearance, and a new face, in unison with nature.

Oranges now should be preserved, and orange wine made. The summer will be found, as mentioned above, in consequence of the diminution of labour for the domestics, the best period for examining and repairing household linen, and for "putting to rights" all those articles which have received a large share of wear and tear during the dark winter days. In direct reference to this matter, that sheets should be turned "sides to middle" before they are allowed to get very thin. Otherwise, patching, which is uneconomical from the time it consumes, and is unsightly in point of appearance, will have to be resorted to.

Employment Services

Employment services ranks among the industries projected to grow the fastest and to provide the most new jobs. Most temporary jobs in this industry require only graduation from high school, while some permanent jobs may require a bachelor's or higher degree. Temporary jobs provide an entry into the workforce, supplemental income, and a bridge to full-time employment for many workers.

Although many people associate the employment services industry with temporary employment opportunities for clerical workers, the industry matches millions of people with jobs, providing both temporary and permanent employment to individuals with a wide variety of education and managerial and professional work experience. Occupations in the industry range from secretary to computer systems analyst, and from general labourer to nurse. In addition to temporary jobs in these occupations, permanent positions in the industry include workers such as employment interviewers and marketing representatives who help assign and place workers in jobs.

Nearly half of all jobs in employment services are at large establishments with 250 or more workers (chart 1). The employment services industry has three distinct segments. Employment placement agencies list employment vacancies and place permanent employees. Temporary help services, also referred to as temporary staffing agencies, provide employees to other organisations, on a contract basis and for a limited period, to supplement the workforce of the client.

Professional employer organisations are engaged in providing human resources and human resources management services to staff client businesses. They also assign workers to client locations, thereby assuming responsibility as an employer while providing a cost-effective approach to the management and administration of the human resources functions of its clients on a contract basis. The typical employment placement agency has a relatively small permanent staff, usually fewer than 10 workers, who interview jobseekers and try to match their qualifications and skills to those being sought by employers for specific job openings.

In contrast to the smaller employment agencies, temporary help agencies typically employ many more workers. Temporary help services firms provide temporary employees to other businesses to support or supplement their workforce in special situations, such as employee absences, temporary skill shortages, and varying seasonal workloads. Temporary workers are employed and paid by the temporary help services firm but are contracted out to a client for either a prearranged fee or an agreed hourly wage.

Some companies choose to use temporary workers full time on an ongoing basis, rather than employ permanent staff, who typically would receive greater salaries and benefits. As a result, the overwhelming majority of workers in the temporary help services segment of the employment services industry are temporaries; relatively few are permanent staff. Professional employer organisations specialise in performing a wide range of human resource and personnel management duties for their client businesses, including payroll processing, accounting, benefits administration, recruiting, and handling labour relations.

Employee leasing establishments, which are a type of professional employer organisation, typically acquire and lease back some or all of the employees of their clients and serve as the employer of the leased employees for payroll, benefits, and related purposes. Traditionally, firms that placed permanent employees usually dealt with highly skilled applicants, such as lawyers or accountants, and those placing temporary employees dealt with less skilled workers, such as administrative support occupations. However, temporary help services firms increasingly place workers who have a range of educational backgrounds and work experience because businesses now are turning to temporary employees to fill all types of positions-from administrative to managerial, financial, professional, and production.

Working Conditions

The average annual work week in the employment services industry was about 32.6 hours in 2002, compared with the average of 33.9 hours across all industries. The low average work week reflects the fact that a temporary employee could work 40 or more hours a week on a contract for an extended period and then take a few weeks off from work. Most full-time temporary workers put in 35 to 40 hours a week, while some work longer hours.

Permanent employees in employment agencies usually work a standard 40-hour week, unless seasonal fluctuations require more or fewer hours. Workers employed as permanent staff of employment agencies, temporary help services firms, or professional employer organisations usually work in offices and may meet numerous people daily. Temporaries work in a variety of environments and often do not stay in any one place long enough to settle into a personal workspace or establish close relationships with coworkers.

Most assignments are of short duration because temporaries may be called to replace a worker who is ill or on vacation or to help with a short-term surge of work. However, assignments of several weeks or longer occasionally may be offered. On each assignment, temporary employees may work for a new supervisor. Employment as a temporary is attractive to many. The opportunity for a short-term source of income while enjoying flexible schedules and an ability to take extended leaves of absence is well-suited to students, persons juggling job and family responsibilities, those exploring various careers, and those seeking permanent positions in a chosen career.

Firms try to accommodate workers' preferences for particular days or hours of work and for frequency or duration of assignments. Temporary work assignments provide an opportunity to experience a variety of work settings and employers, to sharpen skills through practice, and to learn new skills. Nevertheless, many workers in temporary assignments would prefer the stability and greater benefits associated with full-time work.

The annual injury and illness rate for the employment services industry as a whole was 3.6 cases for every 100 full-time workers in 2002, lower than the rate of 5.3 for the entire private sector. Temporary workers in industrial occupations often perform work that is more strenuous and potentially more dangerous, so they may have a higher rate of injury and illness.

Employment

The employment services industry provided 3.2 million jobs in 2002, about 2.2 million of them in temporary help services firms. Professional employer organisations employed 790,000 and employment placement agencies employed another 281,000. Although about 36,000 of the 62,000 establishments in the industry are temporary help services firms, they employ 2 out of 3 industry workers.

Employment in the employment services industry is distributed throughout the United States. Workers are somewhat younger than those in other industries-44 percent of employment services workers are under 35, compared with 36 percent of all workers, reflecting the large number of clerical and other entry-level positions in the industry that require little formal education.

The employment services industry encompasses many fields, from office and administrative support occupations to professional and production occupations (table 1). In general, occupations in the industry include the permanent staff of employment services firms, and the variety of occupations supplied through the temporary help services segment of the industry and the professional employer organisations. The staff of employment service agencies is responsible for the daily operation of the firm.

Many of these workers are in management, business, and financial, and sales occupations, which together account for only about 7 percent of jobs in this industry. Managers ensure that the agency is run effectively, and they often conduct interviews of potential clients and jobseekers. Employment, recruitment, and placement specialists recruit and evaluate applicants and attempt to match them with client firms. Most work in the personnel supply services industry. Sales workers actively pursue new client firms and recruit qualified workers. Because of fierce competition among agencies, marketing and sales work at times can be quite stressful.

About 3 in 10 workers in this industry are in office and administrative support jobs. These positions may be either temporary or permanent. Experience in office and administrative support occupations usually is preferred for these jobs, although some persons take special training to learn skills such as bookkeeping and word processing. Receptionists greet visitors, field telephone calls, and perform assorted office functions. Secretaries perform a growing range of tasks, such as keyboarding and answering the telephone, depending on the type of firm in which they work.

Medical secretaries make appointments and need a familiarity with common medical terms and procedures;

legal secretaries must be familiar with the format of common legal documents. General office clerks file documents, type reports, and enter computer data. File clerks classify and store office information and records. Data entry keyers type information into a computer data base, either through a personal computer or directly into a mainframe computer. Word processors and typists enter and format drafts of documents using typewriters or computers.

Bookkeeping clerks compute, classify, and record transaction data for financial records and reports. Production occupations and transportation and material moving occupations together account for 40 percent of employment in the employment services industry. Many of these jobs seldom require education beyond high school, although related work experience may be preferred for some. Others require significant experience and on-the-job training.

Highly skilled assemblers and fabricators may assemble and connect parts of electronic devices, while those who are less skilled work on production lines, continually repeating the same operation. Helpers perform a variety of mostly unskilled tasks. Labourers and freight, stock, and material movers transport goods to and from storage areas in either factories, warehouses, or other businesses. Hand packers and packagers wrap, package, inspect, and label materials manually, often keeping records of what has been packed and shipped.

A growing number of temporary workers are specialised professional and related workers, who currently account for another 9 percent of employment. Professional and related occupations include a variety of specialists and practitioners, some of whom require many years of postsecondary education to qualify for their positions. For example, lawyers or attorneys generally need 4 years of college and 3 years of law school. They act as advisors, providing counsel on legal rights and obligations and suggesting particular courses of action in business.

Computer programmers write, test, and maintain the detailed instructions, called programmes or software that computers must follow to perform their functions. Other computer specialists include computer support specialists, who provide technical assistance, support, and advice to customers and users. Licensed practical nurses provide basic bedside care to patients. Registered nurses administer medication, tend to patients, and advise patients and family members about procedures and proper care. They usually work in hospitals, but they may be assigned to private duty in patients' homes.

Service workers employed on a temporary basis also include a number of healthcare support occupations. Home health aides usually work in the home of an elderly or ill patient, allowing the patient to stay at home instead of being institutionalised. Becoming a home health aide generally does not require education beyond high school. Nursing aides and orderlies also seldom need education beyond high school, but employers do prefer previous experience. These workers assist nurses with patient care in hospitals and nursing homes. The remainder of the workers in this industry includes those in farming, fishing, and forestry and installation, maintenance, and repair occupations.

Table 1. Employment of wage and salary workers in employment services by occupation, 2002 and projected change, 2002-2012.(Employment in thousands)

Occupation	2002 Employment		Percentchange,
	Number	Percent	2002-2012
All occupations	3,249	100.0	54.3
Management, business, and financial occupations	136	4.2	73.1

Human resources, training, and labour relations specialists	44	1.3	65.5
Professional and related occupations	294	9.0	66.1
Computer specialists	51	1.6	75.2
Architecture and engineering occupations	49	1.5	71.1
Registered nurses	64	2.0	55.9
Licensed practical and licensed vocational nurses	35	1.1	59.3
Service occupations	260	8.0	65.7
Nursing aides, orderlies, and attendants	46	1.4	59.3
Food preparation and serving related occupations	64	2.0	53.4
Janitors and cleaners, except maids and housekeeping cleaners	40	1.2	75.5
Sales and related occupations	92	2.8	63.6
Office and administrative support occupations	924	28.4	47.8
Bookkeeping, accounting, and auditing clerks	45	1.4	43.4
Customer service representatives	71	2.2	75.5
File clerks	33	1.0	27.5
Receptionists and information clerks	67	2.1	75.5
Stock clerks and order fillers	45	1.4	34.8

Executive secretaries and administrative assistants	64	2.0	50.9
Secretaries, except legal, medical, and executive	79	2.4	34.1
Data entry keyers	70	2.2	2.4
Office clerks, general	198	6.1	68.1
Construction and extraction occupations	161	4.9	74.4
Construction trades and related workers	107	3.3	77.4
Installation, maintenance, and repair occupations	42	1.3	73.4
Production occupations	595	18.3	53.0
Assemblers and fabricators	144	4.4	40.5
Metal workers and plastic workers	85	2.6	61.3
Packaging and filling machine operators and tenders	71	2.2	75.5
Helpers--Production workers	99	3.1	40.4
Transportation and material moving occupations	728	22.4	44.1
Driver/sales workers and truck drivers	57	1.8	59.2
Labourers and freight, stock, and material movers, hand	446	13.7	36.1
Packers and packagers, hand	146	4.5	55.9

Training

The employment services industry offers opportunities in

many occupations for workers with a variety of skill levels and experience. The majority of temporary jobs still require only graduation from high school or the equivalent, while some permanent jobs, such as those in management, may require a bachelor's or higher degree. In general, the training requirements of temporary workers mirror those for permanent employees in the economy as a whole.

As the industry expands to include various professional and managerial occupations, therefore, a growing number of jobs will require professional or advanced degrees. Many temporary help services firms offer skills training to newly hired employees to make them more marketable. This training often is provided free to the temporary worker and is an economical way to acquire training in important skills such as word processing.

Agency training policies vary, so persons considering temporary work should ask firms what training they offer and at what cost. Advancement as a temporary employee usually takes the form of pay increases or greater choice of jobs. More often, temporaries transfer to full-time jobs with other employers. Turnover among temporaries within help supply firms usually is very high because few choose to work as temporaries for long; many accept offers to work full time for clients for whom they worked as temporaries.

Some experienced temporaries may be offered permanent jobs with help firms, either as receptionists or in positions screening or training others for temporary jobs. Staff of employment placement agencies and permanent staff of temporary help services firms typically are employment interviewers, administrative support workers, or managers. The qualifications required of employment interviewers depend partly on the occupations that the employment placement agency or temporary help services firm specialises in placing.

For example, agencies that place professionals, such as accountants or nurses, usually employ interviewers with college degrees in similar fields. Agencies specialising in placing administrative support workers, such as secretaries or word processors, are more likely to hire interviewers with less education, but who have experience in those occupations. Staff of professional employer organisations include professionals in human resources management, payroll, risk management, legal services, financial management, employment compliance, and administration.

Although administrative support occupations, such as receptionists, usually do not require formal education beyond high school, related work experience may be needed. Sometimes, staff experienced in administrative support occupations advance to employment interviewer positions. Most managers have college degrees; an undergraduate degree in personnel management or a related field is the best preparation for these jobs. Employment, recruitment, and placement specialists often advance to managerial positions, but seldom without a bachelor's degree.

Earnings

In 2003, earnings among nonsupervisory workers in employment services firms were $13.04 per hour and $425 per week, lower than the $14.95 an hour and $506 a week for all private industry. Earnings vary as widely as the range of skills and formal education among workers in employment services. As in other industries, managers and professionals earn more than clerks and labourers. Also, temporaries usually earn less than workers employed as permanent staff, but some experienced temporaries make as much as or more than workers in similar occupations in other industries.

Most permanent workers receive basic benefits; temporary workers usually do not receive such benefits unless they work a minimum number of hours or days per week to qualify for benefit plans. Less than 3 percent of workers in employment services are union members or are covered by union contracts, compared with about 15 percent of workers in all industries combined.

Employment services ranks among the fastest growing industries in the Nation and is expected to be among those that provide the most new jobs. The industry is expected to gain about 1.8 million new jobs over the 2002-12 projection period. Wage and salary employment in the employment services industry is expected to grow 54 percent over this period, more than 3 times the 16-percent growth projected for all industries combined. Growth in demand for temporary employees fueled the expansion of the industry throughout the 1990s and is attributable to a number of factors.

As competition increased, businesses sought new ways to make their staffing patterns more responsive to changes in demand. To achieve this, they hired temporary employees with specialised skills to reduce costs and to provide the necessary knowledge or experience in certain types of work. Despite recent industry job losses, increasing demand for flexible work arrangements and schedules, coupled with significant turnover in these positions, should create plentiful job opportunities for persons who seek jobs as temporaries or contract workers through 2012.

In particular, suppliers of medical personnel to hospitals and other medical facilities should continue to fare well, as demand for temporary healthcare staffing grows to meet the needs of aging baby boomers and to supplement demand for more healthcare services throughout the country. Employment in professional employer organisations also grew rapidly during the 1990s in response to demands by businesses for changes in human resources management.

The increasing complexity of employee-related laws and regulations and a desire to control costs, reduce risks, and provide more integrated services spurred more businesses to contract with professional employer organisations to handle their personnel management, health benefits, workers' compensation claims, payroll, tax compliance, and unemployment insurance claims. This trend is expected to continue as businesses enter into relationships with professional employer organisations and shift these responsibilities to specialists. Employment placement agencies are expected to continue growing, but not as fast as temporary help services or professional employer organisations.

Growth in these agencies stems from employers' increasing willingness to allow outside agencies to perform the preliminary screening of candidates and the growing acceptance of executive recruitment services. However, online employment placement agencies operate without employment counselors and need fewer administrative support workers. Job postings on employer Web sites; online newspaper classified ads; and job matching Internet sites operated by educational institutions and professional associations compete with this industry, thereby dampening employment growth. Most new jobs will arise in the largest occupational groups in this industry-office and administrative support occupations, production, and transportation and material moving occupations.

However, the continuing trend toward specialisation also will spur growth among professional workers, including engineers, computer specialists, and healthcare practitioners such as nurses. Managers also will see an increase in new jobs, as government increasingly contracts out management functions. In addition, growth of temporary help firms and professional employer organisations-which provide human resource management, risk management, accounting, and information technology services-will provide more opportunities for professional workers within those fields.

Marketing and sales representative jobs in temporary staffing firms also are expected to increase along with competition among these firms for the most qualified workers and the best clients. Following are some tips for tourists. It help the millions of families searching for long-term care choose the best community for their loved ones. Care quality is a vital part of choosing long-term care, yet care quality can change at any time.

Safe and sound: Safety and security features are of the utmost importance. Are the bathrooms accessible and do they have grab bars in convenient locations? How does a resident contact staff if they have an emergency in their room or apartment? What other safety features are available in the apartment and throughout the community? Ask about the staffing schedule to understand who will be on-site to assist the resident. How many licensed nurses or staff members are available? What are the staffing patterns at night versus in the daytime? How are medications managed? If your loved one is prone to wandering due to Alzheimer's or dementia, is a secure unit the right solution?

Care with dignity: As you tour, ask lots of questions about personal care. Look at the current residents. Are they clean-shaven with well-groomed hair and nails? Discuss bathing options and your loved one's preferences. Are the residents dressed appropriately? Is the staff treating residents with respect and a smile?

Clean as a Whistle: Is the community fresh and clean? Look past the furnishings and into corners, baseboards, and windows. Ask how often housekeeping is provided in the apartment or room. What services does maintenance provide? What is their response time?

Follow Your Nose: Odors may indicate lack of cleanliness or just a temporary problem that was caused by one recent incident. If you find odors in a concentrated area of the tour this may indicate a single incident. Odors throughout the community more likely indicate a larger problem. Ask the manager what they believe the problem to be before proceeding.

Busy residents are happy residents: Ask to watch activities. Are they well attended? Does the staff seem to be enjoying the activities as well? Look at the community events calendar. Do the events match your loved one's interests? Look for small and large group activities, trips or outings. Inquire about religious services if this is important to you.

Whistle while they work: Staff attitude and friendliness are of the utmost importance. Observe the staff interacting with current residents. Do they listen and make eye contact? If you feel welcomed while you tour, so will your loved one. Make sure you get a good understanding of the staffing pattern. How many people are truly involved in his/her care? Introduction to the management team will help you understand the goals of the property. Is the manager willing and available to meet with you? Do you have confidence in his/her management style and experience?

Find the great outdoors: Everyone wants to go outside on beautiful spring days. Investigate the outdoor areas for the residents. Does it feel safe and secure? Find out if the staff uses the same area for breaks. Do they host activities such as gardening in these areas?

Choices, choices, choices: The dining room experience is very important to seniors. Discuss entree choices and ask about dining hours and procedures. Bring your loved one in for a meal to taste the food and meet some of the residents. Discuss what happens if a resident cannot make it to the dining room for a meal. Don't forget to ask about the laundry service. Who does the laundry and what is the cost? Ask about laundry procedures.

When it's time to leave: No one likes to move a lot. Ask about specific move-out criteria. Under what circumstances might a resident be asked to move? What type of notice is given; by them or by you? In many cases, a 30-day notice may be required.

Trust your instincts: As you're touring, can you imagine you or your loved one living there and being comfortable? Did you feel at ease while touring? Was the staff friendly and inviting? The property doesn't have to be the most beautiful to be the best place for your loved ones to live comfortably! Follow your instincts and your heart.

Executive Housekeepers

Executive housekeepers inspect rooms for cleanliness and check on other housekeeping tasks to make sure that workers are following proper procedures. They make sure that the work of the housekeeping department falls within the established standards of quality for the hotel. In some establishments executive housekeepers supervise the staff who set up rooms for conventions, banquets, exhibits, and other programmes. Executive housekeepers may be in charge of ordering housekeeping supplies and equipment. They may help in the selection and purchase of new furniture.

Some executive housekeepers work with interior decorators to develop new decorating schemes for rooms and public areas. The housekeeping staff tells the executive housekeeper about damage and equipment that needs repair. Executive housekeepers conduct their own inspections and make recommendations on the relocation of equipment and the use of space. They also develop procedures on how to inform the engineering/ maintenance department when its services are needed. They keep records on personnel, payroll, expenses, and housekeeping activities. They keep management informed about repair work, improvements, personnel difficulties, and expenditures. They submit a yearly budget for review and approval.

In small or medium-sized hotels and motels executive housekeepers may share cleaning chores with the staff. Executive housekeepers who work in small institutions may also be in charge of other operations such as maintenance and ordering food. Housekeepers in hospitals make sure that patients have safe, clean rooms. They follow strict procedures for cleanliness and sanitation to prevent the spread of infection and disease. They develop education programmes for the staff and teach them how to handle contaminated wastes safely. They teach them safety techniques and the correct way to use supplies and equipment.

Staff development is important, and executive housekeepers make sure staff education programmes are ongoing. As a rule, working conditions are very good. Executive housekeepers work in clean, attractive, comfortable buildings. Although they usually have their own office, they spend a good part of their time in other parts of the establishment. They may be on their feet most of the day.

Housekeepers in resort hotels or motels may work longer hours during the tourist season. Executive housekeepers who live in the hotel have regular hours, but they may be on call at any time. Executive housekeepers in hospitals, schools, and other institutions usually work forty hours a week. Salaries depend on the experience and education of the housekeeper and the size and location of the establishment that employs them. According to the Bureau of Labor Statistics, in 2000, executive housekeepers averaged $27,830 a year. Salaries ranged from $7.80 to $20.60 an hour, or $16,220 to $42,850 a year.

Some hotels may offer executive housekeepers and their families room and board and use of hotel services. Other benefits are paid vacations, sick leave, hospital insurance, and tuition assistance for continuing education. At one time the job of executive housekeeper went to the person in the housekeeping department with the most experience or seniority. Today, many executive housekeepers have a college degree or have taken advanced courses in business and management.

Executive housekeepers will have better employment opportunities if they have at least a two-year college degree or have taken some advanced courses in hospitality. They should have a basic knowledge of accounting to keep records and to prepare budgets and reports. A knowledge of labor laws and safety regulations is important. Executive housekeepers may also find it helpful to study sociology, psychology, economics, personnel management and human relations, and communications.

Purchasing, interior design, maintenance and inventory control, basic computer skills, and rules and procedures for sanitation and health may be beneficial. Universities, community colleges, and vocational schools offer programmes that prepare students for institutional housekeeping. These schools may also offer continuing education courses for those already in the field.

Many executive housekeepers belong to the International Executive Housekeepers Association (IEHA). IEHA is a professional organisation with over 6,000 members who work in commercial, institutional, or industrial settings. The International Executive Housekeepers Association has established educational standards for the profession and sponsors certificate and college degree programmes. IEHA also offers numerous self-study courses. Executive housekeepers may also belong to the American Hotel & Lodging Association (AH&LA). AH&LA is a professional organisation with over 13,000 property members who work in the hotel and lodging industry.

Executive housekeepers should be able to communicate well with management, staff, the public, and suppliers. Occupations can be adapted for workers with disabilities. Persons should contact their school or employment counselors, their state office of vocational rehabilitation, or their state department of labor to explore fully their individual needs and requirements as well as the requirements of the occupation. Executive housekeepers work in hotels, motels, condominiums, and clubs. Others work in hospitals, nursing homes, and health-care centers. Some work on college campuses or in schools.

Many of the best jobs are in large cities and their suburbs. A growing number of resort hotels and motels in less populated places also offer excellent opportunities. According to the Bureau of Labor Statistics, the number of jobs for executive housekeepers is expected to increase about as fast as the average for all occupations. The hospitality industry is enjoying moderate growth in the twenty-first century. Some developers are building new hotels and resorts. These establishments may create opportunities for executive housekeepers who are new to the field.

Most jobs will open as workers retire or find work in other occupations. Some large establishments require prospective executive housekeepers to have a college degree in hotel and restaurant management. Others may hire experienced workers who have taken courses in the field. Job seekers may start as floor supervisors, executive assistants, or assistant heads of housekeeping departments.

They learn housekeeping procedures and policies and gain experience managing a staff. In time they may take over the management of the housekeeping department during the late afternoon or evening shift.

Smaller hotels and motels may hire executive housekeepers who lack a formal education in the hospitality field but have worked their way up through the ranks. However, even in these small institutions, the trend has been to look for candidates who have taken some hospitality or business courses. Job seekers may find opportunities at newly built hotels, resorts, hospitals, nursing homes, or other establishments. The International Executive Housekeepers Association maintains a referral service for job seekers and for employers looking for candidates. Since executive housekeepers already hold the top position in their profession, further advancement may be limited.

In many small establishments executive housekeepers may become assistant managers. With more education and experience they may be promoted to become managers. Executive housekeepers in many institutions are considered part of the top management team. Executive housekeepers in chain properties or franchise establishments can advance to positions in corporate executive housekeeping. They may become inspectors, consultants, or specialists in the process of opening new branches.

Bibliography

Beale, Joseph Henry. *The law of innkeepers and hotels: including other public houses, theatres, sleeping cars.* Boston: William J. Nagel, 1906.

Boni, G. de. *Hotel organization, management and accountancy.* London: Pitman, 1939.

Boomer, Lucius Messenger. *Hotel management; principles and practice.* New York: Harper, 1931.

Bradley, Alice. *Cooking for profit; catering and food service management.* Chicago: American school of home economics, 1922.

Dahl, Crete M. *Housekeeping management & organization for hotels & institutions.* Stamford, Conn.: The Dahls, 1945.

______________., and Grace H. Woolley. *Housekeepers' guide to selecting and training employees.* Stamford Conn: Dahl Pub. Co., 1949.

Dahl, J. O. *200 ways to control food costs in quantity cookery.* Stamford Conn: The Dahls, 1941.

______________., *Advertising and promotion for hotels and restaurants; a reference book for hotel and* restaurant executives, sales managers, advertising and publicity directors, advertising agencies, *publishers and students.* Stamford Conn: The Dahls, 1939.

______________., *The efficient waitress manual.* Stamford Conn: J. O. Dahl, 1935.

______________., *Storeroom management and control for quantity cookery profits.* Stamford Conn: The Dahls, 1945.

Dicksee, Lawrence Robert. *Hotel accounts.* London: Gee & Co., 1905.

Fellows, Charles. *The menu maker: suggestions for selecting and arranging menus for Hotels and*Resturants, with object of changing from day to day to give continuous variety of foods in season.Chicago Ill: The Hotel Monthly, 1920.

Hamilton, Francis Frazee. *Hotel front desk management, a treatise on the best methods and procedures in use in small hotels.* Miami, Fla.: Francis Frazee Hamilton, 1947.

Hoke, Ann. *Restaurant menu planning.* New York, London: Harper & brothers, 1940.

Martyn, Charles. *The financial side of hotel keeping.* New York: The Caterer Pub. Co., 1903.

Ogden, Henry N. and Henry Burdett Cleveland. *Practical methods of sewage disposal for residences, hotels and institutions.* New York: J. Wiley, 1912.

Palmer, Mary E. *Guide to hotel housekeeping.* Charleston W Va: The Tribune printing co., 1908.

INDEX